IMAGES OF

UNITED STATES NAVY SUBMARINES 1900-2019

RARE PHOTOGRAPHS FROM WARTIME ARCHIVES

Michael Green

Pen & Sword
MARITIME

First published in Great Britain in 2019 by
PEN & SWORD MARITIME
An imprint of
Pen & Sword Books Ltd
47 Church Street
Barnsley
South Yorkshire
S70 2AS

ISBN 978-1-52674-206-3

A CIP catalogue record for this book is available from the British Library.

Typeset by Concept, Huddersfield, West Yorkshire HD4 5JL.
Printed and bound in India by Replika Press Pvt. Ltd.

Pen & Sword Books Limited incorporates the imprints of Atlas, Archaeology, Aviation, Discovery, Family History, Fiction, History, Maritime, Military, Military Classics, Politics, Select, Transport, True Crime, Air World, Frontline Publishing, Leo Cooper, Remember When, Seaforth Publishing, The Praetorian Press, Wharncliffe Local History, Wharncliffe Transport, Wharncliffe True Crime and White Owl.

For a complete list of Pen & Sword titles please contact
PEN & SWORD BOOKS LIMITED
47 Church Street, Barnsley, South Yorkshire S70 2AS, England
E-mail: enquiries@pen-and-sword.co.uk
Website: www.pen-and-sword.co.uk

Contents

Dedication

The author would like to dedicate this book to
all the US Navy submariners who volunteered to serve
in wartime and peacetime.

Preface

In 1900 the US Navy took into service its first submarine. Named the *Holland VI*, it was 53ft 10in in length and had a surface displacement of 65 tons. The maximum surface speed was 6 knots and submerged speed 5.5 knots. Power came from a gasoline engine on the surface and a storage battery when underwater. Armed with a single torpedo tube and three torpedoes, it could submerge to a depth of 75ft.

During the Second World War, it would be the US Navy's *Gato*- and *Balao*-class fleet submarines that would send the bulk of the Japanese merchant fleet to the bottom of the ocean as well as accounting for a large number of Japanese warships. They averaged approximately 312ft in length with a surface displacement of about 1,500 tons and could submerge to a depth of 400ft.

Manned by a crew of up to eighty men, the *Gato*- and *Balao*-class fleet submarines had a maximum surface speed of 20 knots and 8.75 knots submerged. A diesel-electric drive propulsion system provided power. Armed with ten torpedo tubes, six forward and four in the bow, they carried into battle twenty-four torpedoes and a variety of deck guns.

Jump forward to 1981, when the first of eighteen *Ohio*-class submarines entered US Navy service. At 560ft long and 42ft wide, these had an underwater displacement of 21,000 tons. Manned by a crew of 155, their submerged speed is rumoured to be almost 30 mph. Nuclear-powered, they can remain underwater for decades, surfacing only to replenish supplies. Their main armament of sixteen nuclear warhead-armed missiles has a range of 4,600 miles. Speculation is that the *Ohio*-class can reach a depth of more than 1,000ft.

This 'Images of War' title presents a graphic overview of all the US Navy's submarine classes beginning with the *Holland VI* through to the *Ohio*-class and beyond, both in text and in historical and contemporary images.

Acknowledgements

The historical images in this book are all non-copyrighted US Navy images from a variety of sources. These include the National Archives and the Naval Historical Center. Additional images of US Navy submarines can be found online at www.navsource.org

Images of contemporary US Navy submarines come from various Department of Defense (DOD) image websites. Friends have provided additional images of preserved US Navy submarines. As with all published works, authors depend on many friends for assistance in reviewing their work.

Notes to the Reader

1. Due to the format restrictions imposed by the publisher for this series of books, the amount of detail is not comprehensive. Reflecting the long time span covered by this subject, the author offers only a very broad overview.
2. All weights in tons refer to short tons and not imperial tons.
3. The US Navy often repeated names for individual submarines and class names over their many decades.
4. Design and operational parameters, as well as crew complement, could vary widely over the lifespan of submarine classes and individual vessels within those classes. Hence the information listed in this work for submarine classes and individual submarines represents only a certain point in their service life.
5. Sources do vary on the division of US Navy submarine fleet boat classes. The author has chosen to base his breakdown on the book titled *The Fleet Submarine in the US Navy: A Design and Construction History* by Commander John D. Alden (retired), published by the Naval Institute Press and first printed in 1979.

Chapter One

The Early Years

It took the invention of many crucial pieces of technology for submarines to become practical. The most important was the electrical storage battery (1859), the self-propelled torpedo (1866), and the gasoline engine (1876), followed by the DC electric motor (1886) and AC electric motor (1899). The two men responsible for bringing these technologies together for submarine designs were American school-teacher and inventor John Philip Holland and mechanical engineer and naval architect Simon Lake.

Of these two submarine-design pioneers, Holland won the first US Navy submarine-construction contract because he had the financial backing that Lake did not. The submarine as per US Navy requirements had to be steam-powered for surface-running and battery-powered for underwater-running. Realizing that steam-propulsion was impractical for submarines, Holland abandoned work on a submarine ordered by the US Navy named the *Plunger* and returned his advance payment.

Even before Holland lost interest in the development of the *Plunger*, he had turned his attention to building a series of self-funded submarine designs. The last launched in May 1897 received the designation *Holland VI*. A gasoline engine powered it on the surface, while underwater the submarine operated with an electric motor driven by storage batteries.

The US Navy's First Commissioned Submarines

Impressed by what they saw, the US Navy purchased the *Holland VI* in April 1900 and after a series of successful tests designated the submarine the USS *Holland* in October 1900. It lasted in US Navy service until November 1910. The prefix letters 'USS' before a vessel's name stand for 'United States Ship'.

The six-man *Holland* had a small dome projecting above the hull but no periscope. The only vision the crew had was a small thick pane of glass in that dome. *Holland*'s armament consisted of a single reloadable 18in-diameter torpedo tube. At that time torpedoes were generally referred to as 'automotive torpedoes' or 'fish torpedoes'.

Initially, the *Holland* had two compressed air guns, one on either end of its hull, referred to as 'Dynamite Guns' and later reduced to a single example. The projectiles they fired when the submarine surfaced became known as 'aerial torpedoes'.

Displacement

The US Navy definition of displacement is the weight of water displaced by a warship or submarine. Displacement is a constant for a given water density because the volume (subject to temperature and pressure) is a constant. A 5,000-ton displacement submarine (the weight of water displaced by its hull) can make itself heavier than a surface ship of equal displacement and submerge because it deliberately takes on water ballast.

On the surface, the *Holland* could reach a maximum speed of 6 knots. Underwater top speed was 5.5 knots. A knot is a unit of speed equal to 1 nautical mile (6,080ft) per hour. The *Holland*'s surface range was 230 miles. The vessel was 53ft 10in in length and had a surface displacement of 65 tons.

Simon Lake's Submarines

While the US Navy was considering acquiring the *Holland VI*, the only other design under consideration was Simon Lake's *Argonaut II*. Unlike the *Holland VI*, Lake's submarine lacked any armament and was intended for non-military use only, for example as a tourists' vessel or for locating underwater wrecks.

With the rejection of the *Argonaut II*, Lake went ahead and designed and had built a weaponized submarine named the *Protector* in 1902. However, *Protector* failed to arouse enough US Navy interest for its purchase. He then offered it to the US Army to help maintain the underwater minefields that protected vital American ports from possible attack by enemy warships. The army wanted to order five of them but found itself overruled by the US Navy in a jurisdictional dispute.

First Submarines Class

Pleased with the capabilities of the *Holland*, the US Navy ordered seven improved examples for experimentation and training. All built between 1901 and 1903 and commissioned (taken into active service) in 1903, the seven submarines formed the *Plunger*-class; following naval architecture tradition, the class name came from the first or 'lead' submarine in the series, the *Plunger*.

Unlike the *Holland*, the seven-man *Plunger*-class submarines had no Dynamite Guns but did retain an 18in reloadable torpedo tube. They had a surface displacement of 106 tons and a length of 63ft 10in. Maximum surface speed came to 8.5 knots, while that submerged was 7.2 knots. Unlike the *Holland*, the *Plunger*-class submarines had a periscope that projected upward vertically from the centre of the hull.

The *Holland*'s 'test depth' proved to be 150ft during the US Navy's acceptance trials, during which it had to reach that depth without any leaks or pressure-related failures. Failure to do so would result in the submarine's rejection. Besides the term test depth, there was also a submarine's 'crush depth', which is self-explanatory and based on estimates by the US Navy.

New Submarine Classes

Following the seven submarines of the A-class, the US Navy had an additional seventy-six submarines built before the First World War. They were divided into thirteen classes starting with the B-class through to the O-class; there would be no J- or I-class. The last three submarines built formed what eventually became the T-class.

Between October 1907 and September 1910, the US Navy commissioned eleven submarines divided into three progressively-improved classes: three B-class submarines, five C-class submarines and three D-class submarines. Their surface displacements ranged from 145 tons for the A-class up to 288 tons for the D-class.

Maximum surface speed for the B- to D-class submarines ranged from 9.2 knots to 13 knots, whereas their submerged top speed ran the gamut from 8.2 knots up to 9.5 knots. Test depth for the B-class proved to be 150ft and 200ft for the C- and D-classes. By 1922 all three classes of the submarines had been decommissioned.

The B-class submarines were the first to feature two bow torpedo tubes, with the C-class the first to feature two stern propellers. The D-class variants were the first US Navy submarines with four bow torpedo tubes and the first to have their inner pressure hull subdivided for improved survivability.

E-Class and F-Class

A technological breakthrough that occurred in 1909 involved the construction of two E-class and four F-class submarines. Rather than depending on gasoline engines for surface-running and charging their batteries, they had two diesel engines (invented in 1897). All six diesel-engine-powered submarines were commissioned in 1912 and decommissioned by 1922. The hull classification numbers for the E- and F-class ran from SS-20 through to SS-25.

Diesel engines were more thermally efficient, hence increasing fuel efficiency, which in turn increased submarine range. Diesel engines also offered an added advantage as diesel fuel was far less volatile than gasoline fuel, especially in the confined spaces of submarines. The diesel engines on the E- and F-class submarines were 'mechanically-coupled' to the submarine's propeller shafts, as were the gasoline engines on earlier classes of submarines.

G-Class Through to K-Class

Despite the switch to all-diesel engines on the E- and F-class submarines, three of the four G-class submarines built between 1909 and 1913 were fitted with gasoline engines. These included SS-20, SS-26 and SS-27. Submarine SS-31 came with a diesel engine.

Submarines SS-20, SS-27 and SS-31 were designed and built by Lake. The fourth boat (SS-26) built was based on the design of an Italian naval engineer named Cesare Laurenti and constructed at the William Cramp & Son Shipbuilding Company, the only US Navy submarine he was asked to design.

The US Navy went on to order three examples of the diesel-engine-powered H-class submarines, with delivery beginning in 1911. All were decommissioned by 1922. The hull classification numbers for the US Navy's H-class submarines were SS-28, SS-29 and SS-30.

The Imperial Russian Navy ordered seventeen examples of the H-class submarine from Electric Boat. However, with the overthrow of the Russian Czar in February 1917, not all the H-class submarines were delivered; instead, the US Navy bought six and placed them into service. Their hull classification numbers ran from SS-147 through to SS-152.

After the H-class vessels came eight examples of the K-class, all built between 1912 and 1914. The twenty-eight-man submarines had a surface displacement of 392 tons with a maximum surface speed of 14 knots and 10.5 knots submerged. They had 18in torpedo tubes and a length of 153ft 7in. All were decommissioned by 1923. The hull classification numbers for the K-class included SS-32 through to SS-39.

Living conditions on the K-class submarines and those that came before were extremely unpleasant. US Navy Admiral Charles A. Lockwood commented that 'sanitation arrangements were meagre at best and defied description', a polite way of saying that they stank. At about this time the US Navy's submarines received their favourite nickname of 'Pig Boats'.

L-Class Through to M-Class

When the First World War began in August 1914 the US Navy's most modern submarine just coming out of America's shipyards would be eleven examples of the L-class, built between 1914 and 1917 and commissioned between 1916 and 1917. The hull classification numbers for the L-class included SS-40 through to SS-51. There was no L-class SS-47 submarine.

Besides Electric Boat and Lake, the Portsmouth US Navy Yard, which later became the Portsmouth Naval Yard, received the assignment for building a single example of the L-class submarine to gain experience. Portsmouth had opened in June 1800. In 1914, the same year that saw the beginning of the First World War, the US Navy made Portsmouth responsible for all future preliminary submarine designs.

With a twenty-eight-man crew, the L-class submarines had a top speed on the surface of 14 knots and 10.5 knots submerged. The Electric Boat examples had a length of 165ft 5in and a surface displacement of 457 tons.

Some L-class submarines were the first to feature deck guns, which became a standard feature on all US Navy submarines through the Second World War. They were also the first to have been designed for deep-water operations rather than only coastal operations. Some of the L-class submarines remained in US Navy service until 1923.

The next in line proved to be a single experimental example labelled the M-1. Laid down in July 1914, its commissioning did not take place until February 1918.

When is a Submarine a Boat?

The US Navy's earliest submarines were termed 'boats' rather than ships or vessels (another name for ships). Boats are by definition small enough to be carried by ships. Ships do not carry other ships. Despite the continuing size increase of US Navy submarines from the Second World War up until the present, in the name of tradition, they remain affectionately labelled as boats.

However, it failed to impress the US Navy and performed only as a test and training vessel until decommissioned in 1922. The single M-1-class submarine bore the hull classification number SS-47.

N-Class

Between 1915 and 1917 Electric Boat and Lake built seven examples of the N-class submarines, with some remaining in service until 1926. They were intended only as coastal defence submarines, with their armament consisting of 18in torpedo tubes. The hull classification numbers for the N-class included SS-53 through to SS-59.

The Electric Boat Company examples of the N-class submarines had a surface displacement of 331 tons and a length of 147ft 3in. Top surface speed came out at 13 knots and submerged at 11 knots. The US Navy had all decommissioned by 1926.

O-Class

Based on lessons learned from the design and construction of the L-class submarines, there were sixteen examples of the twenty-nine-man O-class submarines between 1916 and 1918. These were larger, at 172ft 3in, than the previous L-class submarines. The hull classification numbers for the O-class included SS-62 through to SS-77.

The Electric Boat Company examples of the O-class submarines had a surface displacement of 529 tons and a maximum surface speed of 14 knots and 10.5 knots submerged. Some remained in service until 1945 as training vessels. There would be no official P-class submarines.

AA-1 Class

Proposed in 1913 was a class of three experimental submarines that would have ocean-going capabilities and a surface speed of 20 knots to keep up with the fastest battleships of the US Navy in the scouting and interdiction role. The thirty-eight-man submarines became the AA-1 class. The hull classification numbers for the AA-1 class included SS-52 for the first example built and SS-60 and SS-61 for the remaining two examples.

Built by Electric Boat between 1916 and 1919, the three AA-1-class submarines had a surface displacement of 1,106 tons, making them the largest submarines yet built for the US Navy. Commissioned in early 1920, they had a length of 268ft 9in.

Besides having four bow torpedo tubes, the AA-1-class submarines had two trainable torpedo tubes located on their superstructures, one in front of the fairwater and one behind. They could launch torpedoes off to either side of the submarine but not over the bow or stern. The crew had no means of maintaining or reloading them from within the submarine when submerged or on the surface.

T-Class

In July 1920, the three thirty-eight-man AA-1-class boats received the label of 'fleet submarines', reflecting the fact that the US Navy believed that they could sustain a surface speed of 20 knots to work with its battleships. In September 1920, the US Navy reclassified the AA-1-class vessels as the T-class.

To reach the 20-knot surface speed required, the T-class submarines had four diesel engines rather than the two of previous submarine classes. Unfortunately, the T-class submarines could not sustain a surface speed of 20 knots, which was a great disappointment to the US Navy.

The T-class submarines' inability to sustain the required surface speed revolved around design problems with the onboard diesel engine arrangement. Also, due to their size and construction issues, their test depth proved to be only 150ft. The US Navy pulled all from service by 1927.

R-Class

With America's official entry into the First World War on 6 April 1917, the US Navy ordered twenty-seven examples of the thirty-man R-class submarines; twenty from the Electric Boat Company and seven from Lake. Production delays due to destroyers having a higher priority meant that the US Navy did not commission the majority of R-class submarines until after the end of hostilities. The hull classification numbers for the R-class included SS-78 through to SS-104.

Those R-class submarines built by Lake, armed with 18in torpedo tubes, were all decommissioned between 1924 and 1925. These were later scrapped under the terms of the London Naval Treaty of 1930. Some of the Electric Boat examples, used solely for training, survived in US Navy service until 1945.

The R-class submarines built by Electric Boat had a displacement of 574 tons and a maximum surface speed of 14 knots. With a length of 186ft 2in, they were also the first to be fitted with 21in-diameter torpedo tubes, the size of which remained the standard on US Navy submarines up until 1997.

In the US Navy's rush to commission submarines for the First World War, dangerous design short-cuts arose that raised life-threatening concerns. An example appears in a passage from the government publication titled *Building American Submarines 1914–1940* by Gary E. Weir:

> Increasing the size of the submarine force highlighted the fact that vessels were not up to standard, but neither the US Navy nor private industry had satisfactory alternatives. Thus, the US Navy found itself building many types that were seriously outdated, with the most appropriate designs and tasks for future American submarines remaining unclear.

The US Navy's N- and O-class submarines and a few E-class submarines remained along America's East Coast, protecting it from attacks by German U-boats. The US Navy eventually dispatched a total of twenty submarines to the waters around the European war zone, including some from the E-, K-, L- and O-classes. Based in the

Submarine Fairwaters and Bridges

One design feature that evolved with the US Navy's pre-First World War submarine classes proved to be the size of their non-watertight fairwaters built on top of their watertight pressure hull. Until the S-class, the fairwaters on previous classes were kept as small as possible to reduce drag while running submerged.

In the beginning, a submarine's periscope resided in the pressure hull. With the advent of the C-class submarines, a small one-man watertight vertical cylinder containing a periscope appeared within the fairwater, referred to as the 'conning tower'. The conning tower connected to a submarine's inner pressure hull.

As time went on and submarine fairwaters increased in size, so did that of the conning tower, allowing for more personnel within them. Eventually, the conning towers became the attack and navigation centre of Second World War US Navy submarines and the commanding officer's battle station when the boat was submerged.

Another feature that evolved with the increasing fairwater size of US Navy submarines was the addition of a bridge. Initially, US Navy submarine bridges consisted of temporary structures built up on their fairwaters after surfacing. However, these temporary bridges proved to be a hindrance as they took time to erect and to dismantle before submerging.

The temporary bridges' flimsy construction proved unable to deal with the rough seas of the Atlantic Ocean. One solution was to add a waist-high metal enclosure (known as the chariot bridge) at the front of a submarine's fairwater to break up large waves. The first US Navy submarines to have a permanent bridge on top of their fairwater were those of the N-class, with previous submarine classes eventually refitted.

Azores in the mid-Atlantic and at Bantry, Ireland, none suffered destruction, nor did they account for any enemy ships or submarines.

S-Class

Wanting to match the operational capabilities of the German U-boats observed early in the First World War, the US Navy had Electric Boat, Lake and Portsmouth each submit a prototype for consideration, to become known as the 'S-class'.

Lake's prototype designated the S-2 proved unacceptable to the US Navy and was rejected, while those of Electric Boat designated S-1 and Portsmouth labelled S-3 passed initial muster. To meet the number of S-class submarines required by the US Navy, Lake built copies of the Portsmouth prototype. In spite of rejecting Lake's prototype submarine, the US Navy kept it in service until 1929.

Like the three experimental T-class submarines, the role envisioned for the sixty-five planned S-class vessels was as fleet submarines. That called for them to act as scout for the US Navy's battleships and also interdict the enemy fleet before the opposing side's battleships engaged. That requirement called for being able to maintain a surface speed of 20 knots.

Some in the US Navy insisted that the S-class submarines should have a minimum surface displacement of at least 1,000 tons to be considered capable of deep-water operations. Unfortunately available diesel engines could not propel submarines of that minimum displacement at the required surface speed.

The commissioning of the first S-class submarine did not take place until June 1920. In the end, only fifty production examples entered US Navy service, with thirty-one built by Electric Boat, nine by Lake and the remainder by Portsmouth. All had a single 4in deck gun and a test depth of 200ft. Construction of the S-class submarines concluded in 1925. The hull classification numbers for the S-boat class included SS-105 through to SS-162.

Some S-class submarines saw combat following the Japanese attack on Pearl Harbor, Hawaii in December 1941. A few were modernized during the Second World War with radars and air-conditioning. They remained in front-line service until replaced by new classes of submarines in late 1943; some survived into 1945 as training boats. With the end of the war, all remaining examples were quickly decommissioned and eventually scrapped.

Construction Details

Surface displacement for those S-boats built by Electric Boat came out at 854 tons. With a surface speed of only 14 knots, they did not meet the minimum requirements necessary to be classified as fleet submarines. Neither did those built by Portsmouth or Lake.

The diesel engines on the Lake-built S-class submarines proved a great deal more reliable than those of Electric Boat engines that proved extremely troublesome but could still not propel the boats to a speed of 20 knots. In spite of Lake's diesel engines proving superior to those from Electric Boat, any thought of reassigning the balance of Electric Boat's S-class contract to Lake to fulfil was unfortunately out of the question as the latter simply had not the shipyard capacity to build more submarines than it had already committed.

Designations: Part Two

In 1920, the US Navy adopted a letter prefix administration designation system that distinguished between coastal and fleet submarines: the former retained the prefix 'SS' and the new fleet boats received the letter prefix designation 'SF'. These letter prefixes and the many that followed were never painted onto submarines and were merely administration codes.

The S-class submarines had a range of approximately 5,800 miles. The Electric Boat vessels' length ranged from 219ft 3in for the prototype up to 267ft for later examples. Like the previous R-class submarines they had 21in torpedo tubes, while the rejected Lake submarine prototype S-2 had retained the earlier 18in torpedo tubes.

As already mentioned, unlike previous submarine classes entirely designed by commercial contractors to the US Navy's broad requirements, the S-class design came from a US Navy bureau. In spite of this, there remained major design differences between the commercial contractors' products, both internal and external, due to their construction methods and capabilities. The S-class submarines are therefore generally divided into four separate variations labelled Group 1 through to Group 4.

Experimental S-Class Submarines

All the diesel engines in the US Navy's pre-First World War submarines had been licence-built copies of German engines mechanically-coupled to the submarine's propeller shafts. As an experiment S-class submarines S-10 through to S-13 received new diesel engines in 1922. They were copies of those found in First World War German U-boats. Some in the US Navy suggested that the M-1 as well the L-, S- and T-class submarines all be re-engined with the American copies of those same First World War German submarine diesel engines.

To compensate for the poorer-quality workmanship of American industry and its backwardness in metallurgy, the American-built copies of the German wartime diesel submarine engines were de-rated and built heavier to make them sufficiently reliable. In spite of this, there remained severe problems with the poor quality of various engine components such as piston rings, which failed continually.

Diesel-Electric-Drive S-Boats

The US Navy had four S-class submarines S-14 through to S-17 re-engined in 1928 with post-First World War-designed German diesel engines. These in turn drove electric generators that powered high-speed electric motors that turned the submarine's propeller shafts via reduction gears, making them 'diesel-electric-drive' boats. A reduction gear is a transmission employed to bring down the very high revolutions of high-speed electric motors to a suitable rate without causing damage to a submarine's propeller shafts.

The introduction of the diesel-electric-drive propulsion system on the four S-class submarines was the US Navy's first attempt at eliminating the problem of torsional vibration (an angular vibration of an object; commonly a shaft along its axis of rotation) by separating the diesel engines from the propeller shafts. Torsional vibration broke engine crankshafts and generated deafening noise within the submarines. The first realization of what was causing the problem did not appear until the publication of a scientific paper in 1925.

Submarine or Submersible?

In technical terms all the US Navy submarines, whether gasoline-electric or diesel-electric, were submersibles. In other words, they were designed for running on the surface but possessed the ability to submerge for a short duration. A true submarine runs primarily underwater, not a capability any US Navy submarine had until the introduction of the first nuclear-powered boat in January 1955. The term submarine, however, in common usage refers to any vessel that can run underwater, irrespective of duration.

With the diesel-electric-drive propulsion system, the diesel engines in submarines could now operate at more efficient, constant speeds to produce the required amount of power. Their locations in future submarines could also be moved to best suit the US Navy's requirements. These design features made the diesel-electric-drive propulsion systems in submarines very appealing to the US Navy.

The biggest issue holding back the widespread introduction of the diesel-electric-drive propulsion systems in US Navy submarines at that time revolved around the added weight of all the associated electrical equipment, which in turn pushed the displacement of the proposed submarines beyond the accepted limits.

The only thing that would make all diesel-electric-drive propulsion systems feasible in future US Navy submarines would be the development of a new generation of lightweight diesel engines. These would offset the weight of added electrical equipment, keeping new classes of fleet submarines within acceptable displacement limits.

Wartime Influence

Much to the dismay of US Navy officers who had a chance to inspect and test German U-boats following the end of the First World War, US Navy submarines, including the S-class, were obsolete when compared to what German industry had built during the war. The most important advantages of the German U-boats proved to be the clear superiority of their diesel engines and their excellent sea-handling.

To bring the American submarine inventory up to the same level of technology attained by the wartime German U-boats, the US Navy acquired and brought six different examples to the United States in 1919. They were to be extensively tested by the US Navy. Some components were eventually provided to commercial manufacturers to allow them to incorporate their advanced design features into the next generation of US Navy submarines.

The V-Boats

The US Navy had nine submarines built between 1921 and 1934, to test new design concepts and to help define a suitable fighting doctrine. They were generally referred to as the V-1 through to V-9. Not a single class of submarines, the V-boat series consisted of five separate classes of submarines varying in size as well as capabilities. The hull classification numbers for the nine V-boats encompassed SS-163 to SS-171.

The diesel engines on the V-1 through to V-9 were all originally licence-built copies of German wartime designs, most mechanically-coupled to the submarines' propeller shafts. Unfortunately this propulsion system arrangement proved unreliable, as had those on previous non-experimental S-class submarines, due to torsional vibration.

First Three V-Boats

With the thought that bigger might be better, V-1, V-2 and V-3 displaced 2,153 tons on the surface and had a length of 341ft 6in. Because the V-1 through to V-3 submarines demonstrated poor sea-handling characteristics, the US Navy had them decommissioned in 1937. The V-1 had a test depth of 200ft and the V-2 and V-3 a test depth of 300ft.

With the ever-growing realization that America would be drawn into the Second World War, the US Navy had V-1 through to V-3 recommissioned in September 1940. None saw action during the conflict and eventually became training boats. At the end of the war, the US Navy had all of them decommissioned for the final time.

Argonaut *Class*

The fourth submarine in the V-boat series was the V-4 named *Argonaut*. Only a single example entered service with the US Navy in April 1924. It proved even larger than V-1 through to V-3 at 381ft in length with an initial surface displacement of 3,046 tons, making it the largest non-nuclear submarine ever commissioned by the US Navy. It had a test depth of 300ft.

Service employment of the eighty-seven-man *Argonaut* proved disappointing as it exhibited poor sea-handling characteristics due to its large size, as had V-1 to V-3. In 1942, the *Argonaut* had its mine-laying machinery removed and new lightweight General Motors diesel engines fitted.

Besides the new engines, the *Argonaut* also found itself reconfigured as a troop transport submarine in 1942. Sent out on a war patrol minus any additional personnel, it went down on 10 January 1943 while attacking a Japanese convoy.

Narwhal *Class*

The fifth and sixth submarines in the V-class became the eighty-nine-man *Narwhal* class. The class consisted of the *Narwhal* commissioned in May 1930, and the *Nautilus* commissioned in July 1930. They were both in general appearance and size similar to the *Argonaut*, having a displacement of 2,770 tons on the surface and a length of 370ft.

Like the *Argonaut*, the two *Narwhal*-class submarines had new more reliable lightweight General Motors diesel engines fitted in 1942. Both submarines had a test depth of 300ft. Maximum surface speed was 17 knots and when submerged 8 knots. As with V-1 through to V-4, the two *Narwhal*-class submarines proved to have poor sea-handling characteristics. Despite this issue, both went on war patrols, sinking a total of thirteen Japanese ships.

Due to their large size, the *Narwhal*-class submarines eventually found themselves assigned to the role of troop transport, as had the *Argonaut*. For this role, their torpedoes and torpedo-handling equipment were replaced by bunks for up to 120 personnel. Following the war, like most early-generation submarine classes, they were quickly decommissioned for the first and last time.

Dolphin *Class*

Having decided that the large submarines were not performing as well as envisioned, the US Navy opted to bring down the size of the next submarine in the V-boat series, the sixty-three-man *Dolphin* (V-7). It had a surface displacement of 1,746 tons and a length of 319ft 3in. Commissioned in June 1932, it went on three early war patrols before being assigned the training role for the duration of the conflict.

The single *Dolphin*-class submarine retained its American-built copies of German diesel engines throughout its service life. It had a top speed of 17 knots on the surface and 8 knots submerged. In a US Navy manual dated June 1945, the disadvantage of running underwater is described:

> As submarines operate on electric batteries when submerged, their radius is limited by the capacity of storage batteries, and when the batteries run down, the submarine must surface to recharge them by their diesel (surface) engines. At a top speed of 10 mph, a submarine's batteries will be depleted in one hour; at half speed, in four hours; and at cruising speed of 3 to 4 knots, in 24 hours.

Of the *Dolphin*'s four diesel engines, two were mechanically-coupled to the submarine's propeller shafts and the other two were considered 'auxiliary engines' and connected to the electric generators that powered high-speed electric motors. These were intended to recharge the submarine's batteries when running on the surface and as a back-up to provide additional horsepower to supplement the two mechanically-coupled engines. The *Dolphin*, therefore, became a 'composite diesel-electric-drive' boat.

Cachalot Class

In June 1928, the Submarine Officers' Conference endorsed the idea of using the German Navy's *U-135* as a model from which a new class of fleet submarines should derive. The *U-135* had a surface displacement of 1,175 tons and a length of 273ft. Powered by two diesel engines, the forty-four-man German submarine had a maximum surface speed of 20 mph and a range of 12,000 miles.

In September 1930, the US Navy officially proposed that the design of the two *Cachalot*-class submarines in the V-boat series be based on the *U-135*. The *Cachalot* (V-8) came out of Portsmouth and the *Cuttlefish* (V-9) from Electric Boat, respectively commissioning in December 1933 and June 1934.

The Portsmouth-built submarine *Cachalot* initially displaced 1,110 tons on the surface with a length of 274ft. Powered by three diesel engines, the forty-five-man

---

Designations: Part Four

From V-1 through to V-7 the US Navy assigned the vessels the administration prefix letter designation of scout/cruiser submarines 'SC', the letter prefix describing their intended purpose as fleet submarines to serve as supporting vessels for the US Navy's battleships.

In 1931, the V-boats had their prefix letter designations changed to 'SS', except for V-4 that became an 'SM' reflecting its role as a mine-layer, the only submarine in the US Navy inventory ever assigned that designation. The prefix letter codes 'SS' and 'SM' were administration codes only and were never painted onto the submarines themselves.

submarine had a maximum surface speed of 17 knots and 8 knots submerged. Range topped out at 16,156 miles.

Both *Cachalot*-class submarines received power from copies of post-First World War German submarine diesel engines, which had minor problems with torsional vibration but still proved extremely reliable in service. As with the first six V-boats, the diesel engines of the *Cachalot*-class submarine were mechanically-coupled to the boat's propeller shafts.

In spite of the impressive performance of the German-designed diesel engines, the US Navy had the new General Motors diesel engines replace them in the *Cachalot*-class submarines between 1937 and 1938, not wanting to depend on the foreign expertise that could be cut off at any time.

Each *Cachalot*-class submarine performed three war patrols before assignment as training boats in late 1945. Upon the conclusion of the Second World War, the US Navy decommissioned them, struck them from the Naval Vessel Register and eventually sold all for scrapping.

Porpoise Class

The US Navy commissioned two examples of the fifty-four-man *Porpoise*-class submarines, enlarged and improved versions of the previous *Cachalot* class, beginning in 1933. Their hull classification numbers were SS-172 and SS-173. They had a surface displacement of 1,310 tons and a length of 298ft. Test depth was 250ft.

The two *Porpoise*-class submarines, as well as the eight follow-on submarines divided into two classes, also had assigned the general label of 'P-class' as they all proved similar in design. The letter 'P' and their sequence in the series construction appeared on their fairwaters and sometimes on their bows. These would be painted over in wartime. Some pictures show submarine names painted onto the bows.

Powered by four General Motors diesel engines, the *Porpoise*-class submarines had a top surface speed of 19 knots, submerged 8.75 knots. Their maximum range came in at 12,427 miles. Both *Porpoise*-class submarines would go on to perform war patrols before becoming training boats.

As with the four experimental S-class submarines modified in 1928, the *Porpoise*-class boat's four diesel engines connected to electric generators that powered high-speed electric motors that in turn drove the submarine's propeller shafts through reduction gears. They, therefore, fell under the heading of diesel-electric-drive boats, as had the four experimental S-class submarines modified in 1928.

The *Porpoise* class originally appeared with only four submarine bow torpedo tubes. Following the Japanese attack on Pearl Harbor, they had two forward-firing superstructure-mounted bow torpedo tubes fitted. The earlier US Navy V-boats were also upgraded in the same manner. Wartime experience showed these tubes

Air-Conditioning

In 1935, the *Cachalot* (V-8) as an experiment received an air-conditioning system. Tests conducted off the coast of Panama quickly proved that crew efficiency significantly increased. The *Porpoise*-class submarines were the first to feature an air-conditioning system as standard equipment, a design feature that appeared on all the subsequent US Navy submarine classes. Air-conditioning was also eventually retrofitted to the earlier V-boat submarines.

Besides making the life of submarine crews more bearable in warm tropical water, air-conditioning acted as a dehumidifier in controlling the amount of moisture in the air within submarines, which in turn considerably lessened the chances of the onboard electrical equipment being affected.

not to be very useful as they could not be maintained or reloaded when submerged or on the surface.

New Directions

By the late 1920s the US Navy concluded that America's shipyards were incapable of building submarines with the sustained surface speed of 20 knots, the minimum necessary for fleet submarines. In spite of this technical hurdle, those in charge of the US Navy's battleships still insisted that submarines be subordinate to them. Most US Navy submarine officers of the day stated that they would much prefer being allowed to act offensively as independent raiders as the German U-boats had done for most of the First World War.

It was at that time the US Navy began to see Japan as an ever-increasing threat to the United States and commenced looking for a submarine design that had the reliability, range and habitability to operate in the vast Pacific Ocean, with less importance attached to its maximum surface speed. In looking over the various German submarine designs of the First World War, that of the *U-135* acquired by the Royal Navy embodied many of the operational characteristics the US Navy now wanted.

Shark and *Perch* Classes

After the *Porpoise*-class submarines there appeared two of the very similar *Shark* class built by Electric Boat. The *Shark*-class submarines retained the General Motors diesel engine of the *Porpoise* class. They were the first US Navy submarines to be of welded rather than riveted construction. Welding increased their underwater survivability and reduced the amount of oil leakage compared to their earlier riveted-class submarine counterparts.

Following the launch of the two *Shark*-class submarines came six near-identical copies labelled the *Perch* class. Their hull classification numbers included SS-176 through to SS-181. The building of the eight submarines was divided between Electric Boat, Portsmouth and Mare Island. The US Navy wanted all six of the *Perch* class built of welded construction, but Portsmouth proved itself not ready for the changeover and their submarines were of riveted construction.

The Electric Boat examples of the *Perch* class had General Motors diesel engines, those of Portsmouth the first new Fairbanks-Morse diesel engines, and Mare Island the prototype diesel engines from the firm of Hooven, Owens, Rentschler (HOR), licence-built copies of an interwar German engine.

Both the *Shark* and *Perch* class had the same diesel-electric-drive propulsion system as the *Porpoise* class, with high-speed electric motors powering their engines via reduction gears. Unfortunately for the US Navy, this diesel-electric-drive propulsion system remained unreliable, as it had with previous submarines fitted with the same propulsion system. The problem revolved around the technology having not yet sufficiently matured to be genuinely reliable.

Salmon Class

By 1934, the US Navy had concluded that a fleet submarine class of approximately 1,500-ton displacement best met the various operational characteristics sought by the submarine community for service in the Pacific. The result proved to be the first of six examples of the fifty-nine-man *Salmon*-class submarines appearing in 1936. A progressively-improved version of its predecessors, these submarines had a surface displacement of 1,458 tons and a length of 308ft. Test depth was 250ft.

The *Salmon* class would be the first US Navy submarines to be able to reach a sustained surface speed of 21 knots, qualifying it as a true fleet submarine by US Navy definition. By this time, however, the term fleet submarine had ceased to refer to submarines acting merely as long-range scouts for battleships. The US Navy retained the term as a generalized expression for submarines of a certain size and dimensions.

Of the six *Salmon*-class submarines contracted, three went to naval shipyards for construction and the other three to Electric Boat. All six *Salmon*-class submarines were of welded construction, reflecting its proven superiority. Their hull classification numbers ran from SS-182 through to SS-187.

The naval shipyards outfitted each of the *Salmon*-class submarines with four General Motors engines, while those from Electric Boat received power from four HOR engines. The latter eventually proved unreliable and were replaced by General Motors engines in early 1943, which also had reliability problems early on their developmental cycle but these were resolved very quickly. The six *Salmon*-class submarines had the same composite diesel-electric-drive propulsion system as fitted to the single *Dolphin*-class submarine.

Following America's official entry into the Second World War, the *Salmon*-class submarines all performed multiple war tours without loss. By late 1943, as new and improved classes of submarines entered US Navy service, the *Salmon*-class submarines were assigned to training duties. By 1946 all had been decommissioned.

Sargo Class

Taken into US Navy service before the official beginning of the Second World War on 1 September 1939 was the first boat of the six-submarine *Sargo* class, with the US Navy commissioning the first example in February 1939. As with most US Navy submarine classes, the fifty-nine-man *Sargo* boats were merely a progressively-improved version of the previous submarine class. Their hull classification numbers encompassed SS-188 through to SS-193. With a surface displacement of 1,450 tons, the *Sargo* class had a length of 310ft 6in. Top surface speed was 21 knots and submerged was 8.75 knots. Test depth was 250ft. The first four examples of the *Sargo* class built by Electric Boat came with four HOR engines.

The two *Sargo*-class submarines built by the naval shipyards appeared with General Motors engines. Sometime in 1943, the four Electric Boat *Sargo*-class submarines' HOR engines went into the shipyards to have them replaced with the more reliable General Motors engines. All six submarines of the *Sargo* class had a composite diesel-electric-drive propulsion system.

Their Wartime Contribution

Some of the pre-Second World War S-class submarines and the *Salmon*, *Porpoise*, *Sargo* and *Seadragon*-class submarines carried the brunt of the undersea war waged against Japan in the initial part of the war after the attack on Pearl Harbor. From a passage in a 1946 government publication titled *US Navy at War 1941–1945: Official Reports to the Secretary of the US Navy* by Fleet Admiral Ernest J. King:

> During the early part of 1942, while our surface forces were still weakened by the initial Japanese attack of 7 December 1941, submarines were virtually the only United States naval force which could be risked in offensive operations … They made it more difficult for the enemy to consolidate his forward positions … Their operations thus hastened our ultimate victory and resulted in the saving of American lives.

In dry dock after being acquired by the US Navy in 1900 is the *Holland*, the service's first submarine, eventually assigned the hull identification number SS-1. The US Navy paid $150,000 to John P. Holland, the designer of the submarine. It proved not to be the first submarine commissioned into a navy. That honour fell to a French Navy vessel in 1888. *(US Navy)*

A line illustration of the *Holland*. Its inventor, John P. Holland, referred to as the 'father of the submarine', began his working career as an Irish school teacher and self-taught engineer. He did not emigrate to the United States until 1873, aged 32. In 1895, he founded the Holland Torpedo Boat Company to build his submarine designs. *(US Navy)*

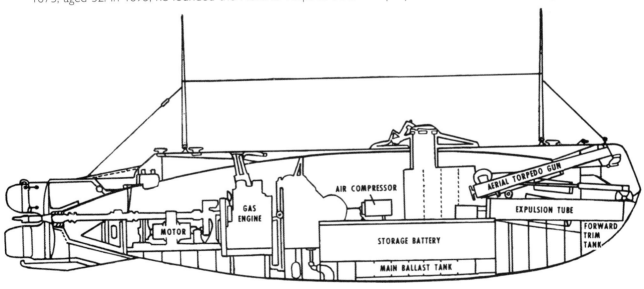

Plan of 53 foot HOLLAND

(**Opposite, above**) Simon Lake, an American-born engineer and business rival of John P. Holland, had also submitted a prototype submarine design for the US Navy's consideration. In this 1898 illustration, no doubt for a newspaper, we see the artist's impression of Lake's prototype submarine named the *Argonaut* sinking an enemy ship. In reality, Lake's submarine had no armament. (*US Navy*)

(**Opposite, below**) Shortly after the introduction of the *Holland* (SS-1), the US Navy commissioned into service seven enlarged examples generally referred to as the 'improved *Holland* type'. The example pictured here is the second constructed. The seven improved *Holland*-type submarines were eventually labelled the *Adder* class. (*US Navy*)

(**Above**) Three of the seven *Adder*-class submarines appear here in dry dock. In 1911, the US Navy dropped class names and submarine names. Hence the seven *Adder*-class submarines became known as the A-class. The submarines themselves became A-1 through to A-7. Armed with a single 18in-diameter bow torpedo tube, they had onboard storage for three torpedoes. (*US Navy*)

(**Opposite, above**) A torpedo goes into an A-class submarine. Robert Whitehead, an English engineer, invented the weapon in 1866. Eventually in 1892, the US Navy placed an initial order of 100 examples of an improved White-head torpedo design. Between 1904 and the 1920s the US Navy depended on torpedoes designed by American Frank M. Leavitt and built by the E.W. Bliss Company. (*US Navy*)

(**Opposite, below**) Pictured here is the bow torpedo room of an A-class submarine, with its single torpedo tube. In the foreground are two reload torpedoes mounted on wooden sleds that were manually pushed across the deck and were aligned to the rear face of the torpedo tube during the reloading process. The torpedoes were ejected from the torpedo tube using compressed air. Once ejected, they travelled to their intended target under their own power. (*US Navy*)

(**Above**) Sailing around New York Harbor is the first submarine in the *Viper* class, eventually reclassified as the B-class in 1911. When the submarine was on the surface, the temporary bridge seen in this image had to be erected on top of the submarine's fairwater and disassembled and stored below before submerging. The concept of a 'crash dive' had not yet been considered. (*US Navy*)

(**Above**) The crew of the C-1, the first submarine in the five-submarine C-class, poses for the photographer. Originally named the *Octopus*, it and the other four submarines in its class were the first to have two propeller shafts rather than the single propeller shaft of previous smaller US Navy submarines. They had two loaded bow torpedo tubes when they sailed, with two reloads stored on board. (*US Navy*)

(**Opposite, above**) The *Narwhal* pictured here would be the first in the three-submarine *Narwhal* class which became the D-class in 1911. Unlike previous submarine classes whose interiors consisted of a single watertight compartment, the *Narwhal* class was the first to have its pressure hull internally subdivided by bulkheads. Another first was the addition of an onboard radio. (*US Navy*)

(**Opposite, below**) The D-class submarines had four bow torpedo tubes. There were no reload torpedoes, only the four loaded in the torpedo tubes before sailing. The submarine fired the same Bliss-Leavitt Mark 3 torpedo that had armed the A- through to C-class submarines. In 1912, with longer torpedo tubes fitted, the C- through to D-class could fire the more potent Bliss-Leavitt Mark 4 torpedo. (*US Navy*)

The two E-class submarines were the first to be fitted with large bow planes, as seen in this old postcard of E-2. The bow planes provided the boats with greater underwater depth control. E-class submarines were also the first fitted with diesel engines for surface running instead of the gasoline engines on previous US Navy submarine classes. (*US Navy*)

US Navy submarine F-4 pictured here was one of four submarines of the F-class. It had two periscopes, a feature that first appeared on the C-class and was eventually back-fitted to the B-class submarines. F-4 sank off Honolulu, Hawaii on 15 March 1915 when leaking battery acid dissolved a portion of its hull; all twenty-one members of its crew perished. (*US Navy*)

Seen here in a railroad boxcar is a diesel engine for an F-class submarine. The engine, based on a German design, was built under licence by the New London Ship and Engine Company (NELSECO), a subsidiary of Electric Boat that was established in 1910. The NELSECO diesel engines generated 780hp and suffered premature main bearing failures. This was resolved in later models. (*US Navy*)

A sailor poses with a periscope inside the control room of an H-class submarine in 1919. Three H-class submarines had been authorized for the US Navy and assigned to American commercial shipyards. The US Navy later bought six additional H-class boats under construction in Vancouver, British Columbia for delivery to the Imperial Russian Navy. *(US Navy)*

(**Opposite, above**) Seen here at the William Cramp & Son Shipbuilding Company is G-4 (or SS-26) of the four G-class submarines. Unlike previous submarines from the drawing boards of Electric Boat or Lake, the G-4 design came from Italian naval engineer Cesare Laurenti. This was his only design for the US Navy. *(US Navy)*

(**Opposite, below**) The G-3 (or SS-31) pictured here at the Lake shipyard was the only G-class submarine fitted with diesel engines. Laid down in 1911 at Lake Torpedo Boat, she had to be moved to New York Naval Shipyard as Lake had gone bankrupt. Finally completed in 1913, the submarine later returned to the reorganized Lake firm for the addition of the hull sponsons seen here. *(US Navy)*

4038 - U. S. SUBMARINE L. 6
MARE ISLAND CAL APRIL 14 1918

(**Opposite, above**) Pictured here is K-8, one of eight K-class submarines. The large circular cap on the upper bow covered a retractable bow plane. Visible on the bottom portion of the submarine's bow is a half-circle cap that rotated to one side when torpedoes were to be fired, marking it as an Electric Boat-built submarine. The cap was designed to eliminate drag generated by exposing the external torpedo tubes. (*US Navy*)

(**Opposite, below**) The L-class submarine, L-6, pictured here is one of eleven examples built by Electric Boat and Lake. The former built seven of them and Lake four. L-6 was designed by Lake and construction subcontracted to Craig Shipbuilding Company. The L-class boats were the US Navy's first effort at fielding an ocean-going submarine. (*US Navy*)

(**Above**) The launching of the M-1 (or SS-47) submarine in September 1915 by Electric Boat. It would not be commissioned until February 1918. It was Electric Boat's first double-hull boat. Note the external individual torpedo shutter doors. Due to design flaws, the boat proved unwieldy when diving or surfacing and hence was considered a failure. (*US Navy*)

(**Above**) In their dress uniforms, the crew of an N-class submarine poses for the photographer. Seven N-class submarines were built: three by Electric Boat and four by Lake. Not intended for open-ocean duty, they served only in the coastal defence role. The N-class was the first with a permanent all-metal bridge, eventually retrofitted to early classes. (*US Navy*)

(**Opposite, above**) The O-9 at its launching by Electric Boat in January 1918. It was one of sixteen O-class submarines ordered by the US Navy. Ten were built by Electric Boat and the other six by Lake. They did not see combat in the First World War but served as training boats during the Second World War. (*US Navy*)

(**Opposite, below**) In this picture we see R-19, one of twenty-seven examples of the R-class submarines. Of the twenty-seven built, the first twenty were constructed by Electric Boat including R-19. The remaining seven boats came from Lake. Rather than having a retractable 3in deck gun such as appeared on previous submarine classes, the R-class had fixed 3in deck guns. (*US Navy*)

7194 - U. S. SUBMARINE R-3
MARE ISLAND, CAL. JUNE 8, 1923

The radio room of an R-class submarine. Built as coastal defence submarines, both the Electric Boat and the Lake versions had four bow torpedo tubes with four reloads. The Electric Boat examples were the first to be fitted with 21in-diameter torpedo tubes, whereas Lake retained the 18in-diameter torpedo tubes of previous submarine classes.
(*US Navy*)

As submarine designs became progressively larger, their fairwaters' size increased, as seen on this R-class boat. US Navy submarine officers had been insisting on larger fairwaters since the L-class, to allow space for an internal conning tower large enough for four men. They finally got what they wanted in the O- and R-classes. *(US Navy)*

Seen here is an example of one of the three experimental A-1 class submarines, eventually re-designated the T-class. All three were double-hulled. Intended as long-range reconnaissance submarines, they could be considered the US Navy's first attempt to deploy a fleet submarine. Inadequate test depth and serious propulsion design flaws that caused premature engine wear and failure doomed the design, but taught designers much. *(US Navy)*

8271 - U.S. SUBMARINES S-14 & S-17.
SEPTEMBER 23, 1924

8338 U.S. SUBMARINE S-14
TORPEDO ROOM - LOOKING AFT.
MARE ISLAND, CAL.

(**Opposite, above**) Pictured here are S-14 and S-17 (or SS-91 and SS-94). Fifty production examples of S-class submarines entered US Navy service between the First and Second World Wars. Designed for use in the Atlantic Ocean during the First World War, they proved too short-ranged to be of much use in the US Navy's campaigns in the vast Pacific Ocean. (*US Navy*)

(**Opposite, below**) A view of the bow torpedo compartment of an S-class submarine. Visible overhead are the tracks for chain hoists used to load torpedoes into the torpedo tubes, or from one side of the compartment to the other. The large vertical tanks on either side of the four torpedo tubes contain compressed air for launching torpedoes from the tubes. The metal racks in the foreground are for storage of reload torpedoes. (*US Navy*)

(**Above**) Looking rearward from the most forward point in the forward torpedo compartment of an S-class submarine, visible are some of the ten reload torpedoes in racks. The sacks on the deck between the reload torpedoes contained provisions for the crew, which were stored anywhere in the boat where there was room. (*US Navy*)

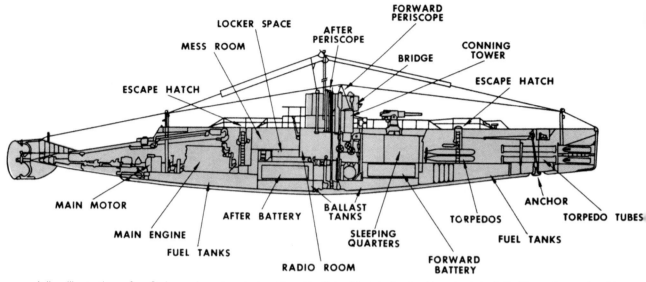

A line illustration of an S-class submarine designed and built by Electric Boat with a single hull. Refrigeration and cold storage units for food made life for the crew aboard these submarines slightly more bearable. The S-boat pictured here has only bow torpedo tubes. Some later S-boats appeared with a single stern torpedo tube. *(US Navy)*

The bulbous bow of this S-class submarine labelled S-2 (SS-106) marks it as Simon Lake's prototype submission to the US Navy as a candidate design for the future S-class submarines. Commissioned in May 1920, its sea trials left the US Navy unimpressed and it therefore proved to be a one-of-a-kind boat. *(US Navy)*

Shown here is the fairwater/bridge of S-46 (SS-157) sometime in the 1920s. Note the sunshade mounted over the open bridge. The wires crossing over the boat's fairwater/bridge and extending to the stern are antenna wires for the onboard radios. The two objects projecting from the starboard side of the fairwater/bridge are running lights for surface running. (US Navy)

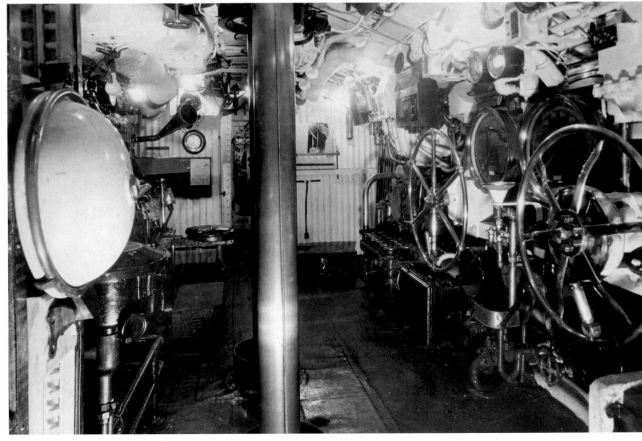

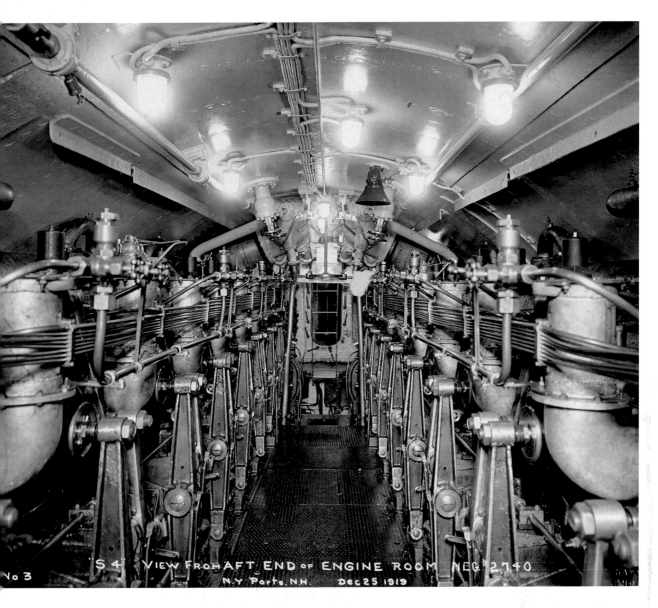

"S 4" VIEW FROM AFT END OF ENGINE ROOM NEG. 2740
N.Y. Ports, N.H. Dec 25 1919
No 3

(**Opposite, above**) With the realization that the German U-boats of the First World War had gone to sea with deck guns of up to 5.1in in bore, the US Navy followed the *Kriegsmarine*'s lead and up-armed the S-class submarines with 4in deck guns seen in this photograph of S-class submarines in the Philippines. (*US Navy*)

(**Opposite, below**) The control room of S-14 (or SS-119) looking aft. In the centre are the submarine's two periscope shafts with their head prisms in their stored positions beneath the control room deck. The large wheels on the right-hand side of the photograph were used to control the submarine's forward and aft diving planes. (*US Navy*)

(**Above**) On the S-14 (SS-119) we see the submarine's two diesel engines. As S-14 was a Lake-built boat based on a US Navy design, it had two Busch-Sulzer diesel engines of 1,000hp each. Lake-built submarines S-3 through to S-13 had two MAN diesel engines of 1,000hp each. Electric Boat S-class submarines had two NELSECO diesel engines that each produced 600hp. (*US Navy*)

Here in dry dock on 22 August 1924 is S-class submarine S-34 (SS-139). Of the fifty production examples in the S-boat class, thirty-one were built with single hulls, meaning the pressure hull was all that separated the crew from the ocean. The other nineteen S-boats were double-hulled, meaning there was another hull, non-watertight, surrounding the inner pressure hull. *(US Navy)*

As an experiment, the US Navy had S-class submarine S-1 (SS-105) modified in the early 1920s with a large water-tight hangar, seen here, for storing a small one-person scout seaplane. Testing of this arrangement was not promising as it took time, necessarily while surfaced, to both assemble and disassemble the onboard aircraft, leaving the submarine very vulnerable to enemy observation and attack. *(US Navy)*

The launch of the Lake-designed and built S-48 (SS-149) took place on 28 February 1921. It sank in shallow water during the builder's trials, but the crew and contractors all managed to escape with their lives. The submarine was eventually salvaged and is seen here brought back to the surface. The boat would be rebuilt and commissioned by the US Navy in October 1922. (*US Navy*)

(**Opposite, above**) In 1927, an S-class submarine managed to ram a pier, destroying its fairwater and the enclosed conning tower. No doubt the incident ended the career of its commanding officer. In 1926 the US Navy decided to lengthen and re-engine some of its S-class submarines to increase their range and endurance. (*US Navy*)

(**Opposite, below**) Here six S-class submarines are moored to a submarine tender in the Philippines in the 1920s. With their short range, the S-class boats found themselves forward-deployed in case of war. One proposal in 1925 was the development of specialized submarine tankers to accompany S-class submarines on patrols. It was not acted on by the US Navy. (*US Navy*)

(**Above**) Some S-class submarines survived long enough to serve in the Second World War, both in combat and a training role. In this picture of S-45 (SS-156) after a refit in October 1943 some of the more modern wartime features are circled, including a new pole mast at the rear of the fairwater that had an attached search radar. (*US Navy*)

(**Opposite, above**) As the interwar submarines came to the end of their service lives, the US Navy began to think about what it wanted in its next generation of submarines. With Japan becoming an emerging threat, the US Navy realized the need for a large and long-range submarine with the endurance to traverse the vast Pacific Ocean. The answer would be the V-class submarine, with V-1 (SS-163) pictured here. (*US Navy*)

(**Above**) The V-class of submarines was a general name for five different classes of boats. In this photograph we see the three submarines of the *Barracuda* class labelled V-1 through to V-3 (SS-163 to SS-165). The high vertical staffs crossed by a T-like structure were for raising and lowering the radio antenna wires that ran from each boat's bow to its stern. (*US Navy*)

(**Opposite, below**) Following the three *Barracuda*-class V-boats was the single example of the *Argonaut* class, V-4 (SS-166). Its role was as a long-range mine-layer. The submarine had two hulls: a watertight inner pressure hull in which the crew resided, and an outer non-watertight hull with the space between used for ballast and fuel tanks. (*US Navy*)

(**Opposite, above**) Pictured here is V-5 (SS-167) of the *Narwhal* class. The only other submarine in the class would be V-6 (SS-168) named the *Nautilus*. Formerly referred to as scout/cruiser submarines, they eventually were labelled fleet submarines. Before their construction, the US Navy wanted them to serve double duty as minesweepers but this was not approved. (*US Navy*)

(**Above**) In this close-up image of the *Narwhal* or V-5 (SS-167), we see its two 6in deck guns and the large superstructure supporting them. A superstructure is the free-flooding framework of perforated light metal and wood built atop a boat's outer non-watertight hull that provides a working deck for the crew when surfaced. (*US Navy*)

(**Opposite, below**) The immense size of the *Nautilus*, V-6 (SS-168), is evident in this image. The openings that run along the submarine's superstructure are limber holes or flood ports. These allowed air trapped within the submarine's free-flooding superstructure (affixed to the top of the boat's outer hull) to escape quickly when the boat began to dive. (*US Navy*)

The poor seakeeping abilities of the *Narwhal* class (V-5 and V-6) led the US Navy to consider a somewhat smaller submarine. The result was the *Dolphin* class, with V-7 (SS-169) pictured here. Unlike the previous V-4 through to V-6 that had a complete double hull, the V-7 had a partial double hull with the torpedo compartments at both ends of the submarine being single-hulled. (*US Navy*)

The US Navy, following the specification of a fleet submarine design, settled on a modified version of a late First World War German submarine class. The result was the two submarines of the *Cachalot* class labelled V-8 and V-9 (SS-170 and SS-171). Pictured here is V-9, named the *Cuttlefish*. *(US Navy)*

In *Cuttlefish's* (SS-171's) control room, an officer plots a course on the chart table that sat on top of the submarine's main compass. The *Cachalot* (SS-170) had a length of 274ft 0.25in and a maximum beam of 24ft 1.25in. Each boat had six torpedo tubes, with four in the bow and two in the stern. Both had a complete double hull, a design feature copied from German First World War submarines. *(US Navy)*

The *Cuttlefish* V-9 (SS-171) is pictured here. Service use of the two *Cachalot*-class submarines convinced the US Navy that with displacement of only 1,100 tons they were too small to be successful as fleet submarines as they lacked the endurance necessary for operations in the Pacific Ocean. (*US Navy*)

In the follow-on *Porpoise* class of two submarines, the US Navy corrected design shortcomings of the previous *Cachalot* class. Displacement rose to 1,316 tons and instead of two diesel engines, each had four. Both *Porpoise*-class submarines had complete double hulls. Pictured here in 1944 is *Porpoise* (SS-172), the first in the class. *(US Navy)*

The US Navy cycled most of its pre-Second World War-built fleet-type submarines through wartime refits, resulting in visible differences as seen in this photograph of the *Permit* (SS-178), a *Porpoise*-class submarine in January 1943. Note the radar antennas for the surface search radar (by the periscope on left) and aircraft detection radar (crossbar atop the pole in the centre). *(US Navy)*

The next fleet submarines following the *Porpoise* class were two *Shark*-class submarines (SS-174 and SS-175). Pictured here is the first in the class, the *Shark* (SS-174). They were near-identical copies of the *Porpoise* class except for partial double hulls and all-welded construction, in contrast to the riveted construction of previous submarine classes. (*US Navy*)

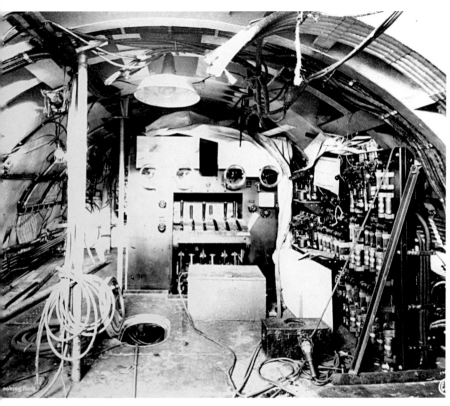

In this image we see the unfinished manoeuvring room of *Shark* (SS-174) of the two-boat *Shark* class. The just-installed manoeuvring control stand takes up the majority of the space. Operators in this compartment controlled the flow of power from generators or batteries to the main propulsion electric motors during both submerged and surface running. (*US Navy*)

Considered part of the P-class were the six submarines of the *Perch* class (SS-176 through to SS-181) with partial double hulls. Pictured here is the *Pompano* (SS-181). The fairwater and bow markings on the *Pompano* reflected its sequence in construction not in the *Perch* class but of the ten submarines falling under the heading of P-class submarines. (*US Navy*)

(**Opposite, above**) On the heels of the *Perch*-class submarines were the six boats of the *Salmon* class (SS-182 through to 187) with partial double hulls. Armed initially with four bow torpedo tubes and four stern tubes, all in the class were eventually fitted with two additional bow torpedo tubes in their forward superstructure, as seen in this picture of *Stingray* (SS-186) in October 1942. (*US Navy*)

(**Opposite, below**) A view of *Salmon*-class submarine *Skipjack* (SS-184), taken in 1938. Rather than having a hull classification number, it retains a letter code representing its class and a number denoting its sequence within the class. This practice continued into early 1939 when they replaced that numbering with the submarine's hull classification number. (*US Navy*)

(**Above**) In dry dock here for painting in July 1941 is the *Sargo* (SS-188), the first in a class of six *Sargo*-class submarines. To reduce crowding in the aft engine room, the US Navy extended it by 2ft. Barely visible are two of the submarine's closed starboard (right-hand side) torpedo tube shutters. (*US Navy*)

In the first official US Navy colour picture that can be dated we see the *Swordfish* (SS-193), a *Sargo*-class submarine, on its launching in April 1939. The entire submarine above the waterline is black and the underside orange. With the advent of war, the fleet-type submarines appeared in an all-black scheme. Eventually they appeared in shades of grey and blue. (*US Navy*)

A view looking into the fairwater/bridge of the second of six *Sargo*-class submarines, the *Saury* (SS-189). It was one of three boats of the *Sargo* class built by Electric Boat, with the other three built by Portsmouth Naval Shipyard. The only external difference between the two sets of submarines was the outline of their fairwater/bridge designs. (*US Navy*)

USS SUBMARINE "BARB"
LAYING OF THE KEEL
June 7 1941
ELECTRIC BOAT CO. GROTON CONN.

Like the previous *Shark*-, *Perch*- and *Salmon*-class submarines, all six boats of the *Sargo* class had a partial double-hull design with the inner watertight pressure hull surrounded by a non-watertight hull evident in this picture of a later fleet submarine. This design layout became the standard for all subsequent fleet submarines. (*US Navy*)

On 23 May 1939 the *Sargo*-class submarine *Squalus* (SS-192) sank off the coast of New Hampshire during a test dive, resulting in the deaths of twenty-six sailors. Thirty-three survived due to a heroic rescue attempt. The painting shows the control room of the boat at the moment when the submarine hit the bottom of the Atlantic in 240ft of water. (*US Navy*)

An artist's interpretation of what took place during the rescue of the remaining crewmen of the *Sargo*-class submarine *Squalus* (SS-192) after their boat sank. The diving bell near the submarine was the relatively new McCann Rescue Chamber. It took 113 days to salvage the boat from the ocean. The US Navy rechristened it the *Sailfish* after repairs and returned it to service. (*US Navy*)

Chapter Two

Second World War

The *Salmon-* and *Sargo*-class fleet submarines would prove very popular with the US Navy submarine community and they confirmed that the decision to settle on a submarine class of approximately 1,500-ton displacement was the correct choice. With the design parameters set, the US Navy commissioned more than 200 examples of very similar fleet-class submarines between 1939 and 1945. These were divided into five classes: the *Seadragon*, *Tambor*, *Gato*, *Balao* and *Tench*.

Seadragon Class

The *Seadragon*-class submarines, near-identical copies of the *Sargo* class, were commissioned following the official beginning of the Second World War, the first of these in October 1939 and the last in December 1939. Their hull classification numbers ran from SS-194 to SS-197.

All four examples of the *Seadragon* class had a diesel-electric-drive propulsion system with high-speed electric motors powering their engines via reduction gears. It was this now mature diesel-electric-drive propulsion system that became standard on all subsequent US Navy submarine fleet classes through the Second World War, as well as those of the early Cold War period.

With a surfaced displacement of 1,450 tons, the *Seadragon*-class submarines had a length of 310ft 6in with a pre-war crew complement of fifty-five that rose to seventy-eight men during the Second World War. The rise in the number of crewmen on board the submarine during the Second World War also occurred with other pre-war US Navy fleet submarines that saw service in the conflict.

Tambor Class

Commissioned between June 1940 and June 1941 were twelve examples of the *Tambor*-class submarines, a refined version of the previous *Sargo*- and *Seadragon*-class submarines with a crew of sixty. The *Tambor* class's most significant departure from all previous classes' armament was six internal bow torpedo tubes rather than four. This supported more shots without reloading, as well as stowage for two more torpedoes. Complementing the six in the bow were four stern tubes, a feature first appearing on the AA-1 class.

Another weapon first appearing on the *Tambor* class and available for deployment from all following fleet submarine classes were two underwater mines that deployed from the boat's torpedo tubes. Their designations were the Mk. 10 and Mk. 12. However, the post-war US Navy submarine community decided that the mines had not been worth the effort as they officially accounted for only five Japanese ships.

Five of the twelve *Tambor*-class submarines were from Electric Boat and the remaining seven from US Navy yards including Portsmouth and Mare Island. Those submarines constructed by Portsmouth and Mare Island received the nickname 'Government Boats' or 'Portsmouth Boats', even if built by Mare Island.

The *Tambor*-class submarines from Electric Boat had lightweight diesel engines supplied by General Motors and those from the naval yards had lightweight Fairbanks-Morse diesel engines. The *Tambor*-class hull classification numbers ran from SS-198 to SS-203, minus hull classification numbers SS-204 and SS-205 applied to another submarine class.

Seven *Tambor*-class submarines went down in combat. Offsetting those losses was the *Tambor*-class submarine SS-199 that sank twenty-six Japanese ships during the war. After hard use, the five remaining *Tambor*-class submarines became training boats until decommissioned following the surrender of Japan in September 1945.

Mackerel Class

As an experiment, the US Navy had two small and short-ranged thirty-seven-man non-fleet-class submarines commissioned, the *Mackerel* (SS-204) in March 1941, and the *Marlin* (SS-205) in August 1941. The former came out of Electric Boat and the latter Portsmouth. The *Mackerel* had a length of 243ft 1in and a surface displacement of 800 tons.

With a diesel-electric-drive propulsion system, the *Mackerel*-class submarines had a top surface speed of 16 knots and when submerged 11 knots. Armament consisted of six torpedo tubes (four in the bow and two in the stern), plus a 3in deck gun.

There were a couple of reasons for the *Mackerel*-class submarines' construction. One revolved around a US Navy fear, expressed in 1934, that if war came then large fleet-type submarines could not be mass-produced. (This proved incorrect.) Another came from a senior officer in the submarine community who believed as late as 1936 that small submarines, about the size of the interwar-commissioned S-class submarines, could play an important role in wartime.

Fortunately, wiser heads prevailed and no additional *Mackerel*-class submarines came out of America's shipyards. Neither *Mackerel* nor *Marlin* saw combat, serving only as platforms for experiments and as training boats. Both found themselves quickly decommissioned after the Second World War.

Gato Class

The next progressively-improved fleet submarines after the *Tambor* class comprised seventy-seven examples of the *Gato* class. The first was commissioned in November 1941 and assigned the name *Drum* (SS-228). The lead ship of the class, *Gato* (SS-212) from which the class received its name was not commissioned until the very end of December 1941, after the attack on Pearl Harbor. The last *Gato*-class submarine commissioned was the *Croaker* (SS-246) in April 1944.

The *Gato*-class hull classification numbers ran from SS-206 through to SS-364. The hull classification numbers assigned to US Navy submarines did not always reflect the sequence in which the boats were laid down (construction began) or commissioned. Due to the large number of *Gato*-class submarines ordered, the US Navy had to abandon the tradition of assigning each submarine in the class a name beginning with the first letter of the class name.

Wartime Submarine-Builders

With America's official entry into the Second World War, the US Navy fixed the design of the *Gato* class. To accelerate delivery of *Gato*-class submarines, the Manitowoc Shipbuilding Company on the Great Lakes joined the submarine-building shipyards of Portsmouth, Mare Island and Electric Boat. Manitowoc built its *Gato*-class submarines to the Electric Boat blueprints and sent its boats down the Mississippi River to reach the ocean instead of east to the Saint Lawrence Seaway.

To increase production of the *Gato*-class submarines the US Navy also brought into the programme the William Cramp & Son Shipbuilding Company. The original firm had opened in 1830 but had gone out of business in 1926. It was re-opened in 1940 under new management which retained the original name of the firm. Assigned to build twenty-nine boats to be based on Portsmouth blueprints, it managed to only complete ten submarines before the war concluded due to poor management practices and a lack of skilled workers. The remainder had to be finished by other shipyards.

Due to a shortage of lightweight General Motors and Fairbanks-Morse diesel engines, some of the *Gato* class went to sea with the troublesome HOR diesel engines. Despite efforts to correct their initial design deficiencies, the HOR engines continued to be unreliable on the *Gato*-class submarines so equipped and were eventually replaced with General Motors and Fairbanks-Morse diesel engines.

Description

While the *Tambor* class had a surface displacement of 1,499 tons and a length of 307ft 2in, the *Gato* class had a surface displacement of 1,523 tons and a length of 311ft 8in. The increased size and length of the *Gato* class provided enhanced stability, and space to subdivide the boats' four diesel engines into two separate compartments rather than the one of the previous *Tambor*-class submarines. It also improved the survivability of the *Gato*-class submarines by providing a degree of redundancy if one engine room became disabled due to a depth-charge attack, for example.

From a US Navy manual on fleet submarines dated June 1946 comes this passage describing the inner pressure hull layout of the *Gato*-class submarines:

> It is divided into eight watertight compartments, separated by pressure bulk-heads provided with watertight pressure-resisting doors. The ninth compartment, the conning tower, in the shape of a cylinder placed on its side, is located above the control room [in the fairwater] and connects with the control room [in the hull] through an access hatch.

In December 1940 the US Navy subjected three of the *Tambor*-class submarines to a series of depth-charges, uncovering design weaknesses corrected in the *Gato* class. In the light of combat experience, the US Navy increased the class's test depth to 300ft, 50ft deeper than any previous class, and estimated a crush depth of 500ft.

Gato-class submarines arrived in the Pacific Theatre in mid-1942, with thirteen in service at the end of the year. In 1943 there were thirty-seven in the Pacific, and by 1944 a total of sixty-four. In 1945, the number dropped to fifty-nine due to losses and damage. Of the 1,635 war patrols made by US Navy submarines in the Pacific Theatre, 587 were conducted by *Gato*-class submarines (34 per cent of the total).

Of the seventy-seven *Gato*-class submarines constructed, twenty were lost to combat action, one of which was claimed by a Japanese submarine. In return, *Gato*-class submarines accounted for four Japanese submarines as well as a multitude of Japanese warships and merchant ships.

Balao Class

In a continuing series of design improvements made to the *Gato* class, there eventually appeared an improved version labelled the *Balao* class. Some 108 units went into service before the end of the Second World War, the first in February 1943; another 12 came out of the shipyards in the immediate post-war period.

In Combat with the *Balao* Class

An example of a *Balao*-class submarine in action appears in the Medal of Honor citation of Commander Richard O'Kane. He was the highest-scoring US Navy submarine commander during the Second World War, credited with sinking thirty-one enemy ships, as well as the most enemy ships sunk during a single war patrol totalling ten, while in command of the *Tang* (SS-306):

For conspicuous gallantry and intrepidity at the risk of his life above and beyond the call of duty as commanding officer of the USS *Tang* operating against two enemy Japanese convoys on 23 and 24 October 1944, during her fifth and last war patrol. Boldly maneuvering on the surface into the midst of a heavily escorted convoy, Commander O'Kane stood in the fusillade of bullets and shells from all directions to launch smashing hits on three tankers, coolly swung his ship to fire at a freighter and, in a split-second decision, shot out of the path of an onrushing transport, missing it by inches. Boxed in by blazing tankers, a freighter, transport, and several destroyers, he blasted two of the targets with his remaining torpedoes and, with pyrotechnics bursting on all sides, cleared the area.

Twenty-four hours later, he again made contact with a heavily escorted convoy steaming to support the Leyte campaign with reinforcements and supplies and with crated planes piled high on each unit. In defiance of the enemy's relentless fire, he closed the concentration of ship and in quick succession sent two torpedoes each into the first and second transports and an adjacent tanker, finding his mark with each torpedo in a series of violent explosions at less than 1,000-yard range. With ships bearing down from all sides, he charged the enemy at high speed, exploding the tanker in a burst of flame, smashing the transport dead in the water, and blasting the destroyer with a mighty roar which rocked the *Tang* from stem to stern. Expending his last two torpedoes into the remnants of a once powerful convoy before his own ship went down, Commander O'Kane, aided by his gallant command, achieved an illustrious record of heroism in combat, enhancing the finest traditions of the U.S. Naval Service.

The primary differences between the majority of the *Balao* class and the previous *Gato* class were internal. The most important was the adoption of high-tensile steel (HTS) in the construction of the *Balao*-class inner pressure hull and watertight conning tower. The *Balao*-class hull classification numbers ran from SS-285 through to SS-428, with twelve examples within that hull classification range cancelled.

Stronger and thicker than the mild steel used for all previous submarine inner pressure hulls, HTS brought the *Balao* class's test-depth down to 400ft and crush test depth to 600ft. This significantly increased the number of depth-charges required in an attack by enemy ASW assets to destroy a *Balao*-class submarine.

The addition of HTS to the *Balao*-class submarines was kept secret from most, and those who did know began referring to the *Balao* class as 'thick skins' and the previous *Gato* class as 'thin skins'. Some of the early-production *Balao*-class submarines built at Manitowoc went into service with mild steel as the HTS had not yet been delivered.

About halfway through the *Balao* class production run, torpedo stowage was increased to twenty-eight, an increase of four over the *Gato* class. The *Balao* class incorporated many if not all the external changes made to the *Gato* class from combat experience, the most noticeable being the continuing reduction in the size of the fairwater to make the boats less conspicuous when on the surface.

Tench Class

Combat experience in the Second World War highlighted the underwater noise generated by the combination of high-speed electric motors and the reduction gears that drove the propellers. The noise sometimes gave away a submarine's submerged location to Japanese ASW vessels. Even if a boat when attacked was not lost, depth-charging could cut short its patrol and necessitate a delay in a yard for repairs, weaken the boat and increase the risk of subsequent loss, or injure or kill crewmen.

The eventual answer to the noise problem was the development of heavy-duty low-speed electric motors mounted that directly drove the submarine's propeller shafts. First retrofitted to the *Sea Owl*, a *Balao*-class submarine, all the *Tench*-class boats used direct-drive propulsion, greatly reducing the noise. *Tench* (SS-417), laid down on 1 April 1944 and launched on 7 July 1944 – underscoring the speed with which submarines came out of the shipyards – had its commissioning on 6 October 1944.

The US Navy authorized a total of 147 *Tench*-class submarines for construction in 1943. However, with the US Navy's conclusion in 1943 that it would have sufficient fleet submarines to see the war through, only twenty-seven examples of the *Tench* class were commissioned before the Japanese surrender in August 1945.

The *Tench*-class hull classification numbers ran from SS-417 through to SS-525 with twenty-five examples within that range cancelled, as were as all those with hull classification numbers beginning with SS-526 and above.

Underwater Weaponry

The most common torpedo employed by US Navy submarines during the Second World War bore the designation Mk. 14. Design work on it began in 1931 and it entered service in 1938. With a diameter of 21in, the 3,280lb torpedo had a length of 20ft 6in and was labelled an air-steam (steam-turbine) torpedo. By this time torpedoes had the nickname 'tin fish' or just 'fish'.

The two-speed Mk. 14 could obtain a maximum speed of 46 knots with a range of 3,500 yards. When running at a reduced speed of 31.5 knots, the maximum range could be as much as 9,000 yards. Most wartime attacks by US Navy submarines employing the Mk. 14 had the torpedo set for high-speed running, giving the intended target(s) less time to detect the torpedo wake or submarine and take evasive action. This also lessened the number of errors due to target course and speed estimation.

Combat experience revealed that the optimum range for engaging enemy merchant ships with the Mk. 14, once the design defects were addressed, was slightly below 1,500 yards. At less than 1,000 yards torpedo accuracy fell off due to fire-control errors. The same occurred with torpedoes fired from over 3,000 yards.

A wartime shortage of the Mk. 14 existed because of the very high expense of the torpedoes themselves, the flawed pre-war doctrine that impacted forecast demand, the loss of hundreds of Mk. 14 torpedoes in the Japanese attack on the US Navy base at Cavite in the Philippines in the opening of the war, and inadequate provision of production capacity. A partial solution revolved around doing away with the capacity for a long-range, slow-speed run on the Mk. 14, which speeded up production. The modified Mk. 14 received the designation Mk. 23.

Before the Mk. 14 there was the smaller and slower Mk. 10 steam-turbine torpedo introduced into service in 1918 for the R- and S-class submarines, arriving too late to see service in the First World War. Its top speed was 36 knots and it had a warhead of approximately 500lb. Due to early-war problems with the Mk. 14 and an ongoing shortage that persisted until the beginning of 1945, the Mk. 10 remained in service until almost the end of the Second World War.

The US Navy had anticipated in 1939 it would take seven torpedoes to sink an enemy battleship, but only one for a merchant ship. The US Navy also predicted that its submarines would enjoy a success rate of 75 per cent when firing torpedoes at enemy ships. Post-war studies showed that US Navy submarines only struck their intended targets with torpedoes 33 per cent of the time.

Description

The Mk. 14 consisted of four main sections: the 4ft-long head that eventually contained a 643lb warhead and an exploder mechanism to detonate it at the chosen moment; behind it, the largest portion of the torpedo, approximately 4ft, contained the torpedo's propulsion system; the torpedo's afterbody included the propulsion and steering mechanisms; and at the extreme rear of the torpedo were four fins and two vertical rudders and propeller.

The vital parts of the Mk. 14 torpedo's steering mechanism in the afterbody consisted of the onboard gyro and the depth-keeping mechanism. How the gyro guided a torpedo to its intended target appears in a US Navy post-war manual:

> During a torpedo's run, the axis of the spinning gyro remains rigid in space; that is, it points constantly in the same direction. If the torpedo turns off its set course, the gyro axis will still point in its original direction. That means that when

the torpedo turns off course, the gyro will be in a different position relative to the rest of the torpedo. The steering mechanism detects this difference and sends correcting orders to the steering engine. The steering engine then turns the steering rudders to bring the torpedo back on course.

The supposed advantage imparted by the onboard gyro in the Mk. 14, and the previous Mk. 10, was the ability to fire at an offset angle of up to 90 degrees, meaning in theory that a US Navy submarine could fire a salvo or 'spread' of torpedoes at an enemy ship without having its bow or stern torpedo tubes directly facing the vessel.

From a US Navy manual appears this description of the three types of torpedo spread employed by submarine commanders when engaging enemy ships:

1. Longitudinal spread. A pattern formed by firing a succession of torpedoes along a practically identical track. The submarine steers a constant course and uses the same periscope and gyro angles, but fires at different points of aim on the same target.
2. Divergent spread. A fan-like pattern formed by a succession of torpedoes fired at the same point of aim but with gyros set to such angles that torpedoes cross the target track at different points. This is not to be confused with the change in gyro angles necessary to make all torpedoes of a salvo hit the target at the same point.
3. Parallel spread. A pattern formed by firing torpedoes simultaneously from bow and stern tubes with gyro angles set so that the torpedoes run parallel.

By 1930, the US Navy submarine community had concluded that the process of trying to fire torpedoes at an offset angle proved too complicated to be practical. Development before the Second World War of the Torpedo Data Computer or TDC, an electro-mechanical fire-control computer, made offset-angle firing a realistic option. Despite that ability, few submarine commanders took advantage of it during combat.

Problems with the Mk. 14 Torpedo

Whereas the Mk. 10 had a simple contact exploder, the Mk. 14, developed during the interwar period in great secrecy, had been provided with a state-of-the-art magnetic influence exploder. In theory, as the torpedo passed underneath the unarmoured keel of a warship the magnetic field of the ship would set off its magnetic influence exploder. The resulting explosion would form a massive air bubble that, upon collapsing, would break the ship's keel.

Unfortunately, budget limitations coupled with secrecy surrounding the Mk. 14's magnetic influence exploder discouraged any realistic testing. The torpedo would not even be issued to the US Navy's submarines until the attack on Pearl Harbor for fear of a security breach. The result was, as stated by author Theodore Roscoe in his book titled *United States Submarine Operations in World War Two*, 'The US Navy entered the war with an entire generation of submarine personnel who had never seen nor heard the detonation of a submarine torpedo.'

As could have been predicted, the unproven Mk. 14 and its Mk. 6 exploders proved to be a dismal failure in combat, resulting in few enemy ships sunk. The torpedoes either passed harmlessly under the enemy ships or went off prematurely before even coming close to their chosen target.

Issues with the Mk. 14's magnetic influence exploder soon appeared in numerous reports by US Navy submarine commanders documenting its shortcomings. An example appeared in *War Report April 14, 1942–June 3, 1942* by Lieutenant Commander J.W. Coe of the *Skipjack* (SS-184) a *Salmon*-class submarine. In his report he stated: 'What we on the submarine firing line need is a dependable torpedo; and at least the knowledge of what the fish [torpedo] will or will not do; when we have this some of those Jap ships which "got away" will start going to the bottom.'

Looking for a Solution

Even when the submarine crews disabled the Mk. 14 magnetic influence exploder and relied only on its back-up contact detonator, they still failed to sink Japanese ships. The US Navy was unaware that the depth-keeping mechanism on the Mk. 14 was misdesigned and miscalibrated, running 11ft deeper than set.

Even after the depth settings were raised on the Mk. 14 and strikes occurred, torpedoes failed to explode except in glancing blows. The contact exploder's movement was impeded by friction caused by inertia, weakening the force with which it was to have struck the firing cap.

Those at the Bureau of Ordnance, some of the most senior US Navy personnel, as well as those at the Newport Torpedo Station, blamed the failures on the submariners. While the weapon was complex – a design too complex for practical use in the field, perhaps a greater failing – their indifference meant that the men at the sharp point of the spear lacked an effective, trustworthy torpedo for nearly half of the Second World War. Immeasurable is the number of American submariners who lost their lives because of it.

Only when a massive volume of evidence became available and Admiral Ernst King, Chief of Naval Operations intervened, were the problems finally corrected by early 1944. The result was a dramatic increase in the sinking of Japanese ships. In 1942, US Navy submarines sank only 134 enemy ships; by 1944 that number rose to 492 ships. By the war's end, a total of 12,000 Mk. 14 torpedoes came out of America's factories. It remained in use by US Navy submarines until the 1970s.

New Torpedoes

The steam turbine engines on the Mk. 10 and Mk. 14 left a trail of exhaust bubbles on the surface as they travelled underwater to their intended targets. In daylight operations, concern arose over sharp-eyed enemy lookouts spotting the trail of bubbles and having their ships taking evasive action.

The other concern revolved around fast-moving enemy ASW vessels following the trail of exhaust bubbles generated by the Mk. 10 and Mk. 14 back to the underwater location of the US Navy submarines that fired them. To solve this problem there appeared a requirement for a wakeless torpedo.

Developmental work on a wakeless torpedo for US Navy submarines had initially begun in 1915 but had ended in 1918 without success. In the immediate aftermath of the First World War, American industry copied a captured German wartime electric (battery-powered) torpedo, which became the Mk. 20 but never went into production.

In 1943, there appeared an American industry copy of a captured German Second World War electric torpedo assigned the designation Mk. 18. It proved highly successful and accounted for 65 per cent of all torpedoes fired by US Navy submarines in 1945 and an estimated million tons of Japanese shipping. The Mk. 18 remained in the US Navy inventory until the 1950s.

Late-War Torpedoes

Another wartime US Navy torpedo turned out to be the very specialized Mk. 27. It was a homing torpedo with an onboard sonar system in its nose section. Nicknamed the 'Cutie', it provided submarines with the ability to engage attacking ASW vessels. The 106 Mk. 27 torpedoes launched in the latter part of the war in the Pacific sank twenty-four enemy ships and damaged another nine. The wartime German submarines had a counterpart, but the Japanese Navy did not see fit to develop one.

At the very end of the war in the Pacific, the US Navy introduced into submarine service the Mk. 28. It consisted of a modified Mk. 14, with an electric motor from the Mk. 18 and the sonar-equipped nose from the Mk. 27. Only fourteen were fired, with four hits on enemy vessels reported.

Hitting the Target

An electro-mechanical fire-control computer labelled the Torpedo Data Computer (TDC) aided US Navy submarine commanders in tracking and engaging enemy ships. Work on the device had begun in the early 1930s, with a prototype appearing in 1938. In its final form, designated the Mk. 3, it went into all the wartime US Navy submarines and remained in the vessels until replaced in the 1950s.

Before the advent of the TDC, the fire-control problem (how to successfully deduce the bearing and speed of an enemy ship before firing a torpedo) involved a great many mental computations by a submarine's commanding officer to solve the relative motion problem. To assist him in those mental computations he and another officer had a hand-held, slide-rule-type calculator referred to as the 'Is-was' or 'Banjo'.

When in operation the TDC would continually point a submarine's torpedoes at a target as the fire-control problem developed in real time. The TDC mechanically generated a continuous picture of changing submarine motion and target motion. It then electrically set spindle settings in the torpedo while still in its torpedo tube, providing the projected target's bearing at firing. Its wartime Japanese and German counterparts were unable to track targets continuously.

The input for the TDC came from a variety of onboard sources. Bearings, the line-of-sight direction from the submarine to the intended target, came from the Target Bearing Transmitter (TBT) when on the surface and from a periscope when running submerged. Radar or active sonar was also used to acquire a targeted ship's bearing. However, the use of radar and active sonar could divulge a submarine's presence to enemy ships equipped with electronic emission detection gear.

Radar

A variety of electronic sensors became standard equipment on US Navy wartime fleet submarines. For warning of approaching aircraft, there was an air-search radar assigned the designation 'SD' in late 1941. It had a range of approximately 6 to 10 miles. It did not provide an aircraft's altitude, only its range. It gave at most a minute's notice of an attacking aircraft, and allowed the crew to distinguish aircraft not closing on the submarine. Its replacement appeared in early 1945 and had the designation 'SV'. Whereas the earlier SD operated on the surface, the SV would function with a submarine running at periscope depth.

The second piece of radar equipment appeared in August 1942: a surface search radar 'SJ'. It had a reliable range of 10 miles but could on occasion pick up contacts at a range of up to 20 miles. Its adoption allowed US Navy submarines to track and engage enemy ships in surface night attacks, which soon became the preferred method of attack. Its efficiency improved with the later addition of a Plan Position Indicator (PPI) scope inside the submarines.

An improved surface search radar received the designation 'ST' and began appearing in 1944. It, in turn, was partially replaced very late in the war by a surface search radar labelled the 'SS' but only on very late-war submarines.

To detect airborne radars fitted to enemy aircraft, the US Navy adopted a US Army-developed and fielded radar detector labelled the 'APR-1'; in US Navy service it became the 'SPR-1'. There also appeared on late-war US Navy submarines another radar detector, the 'SPR-2', which focused on identifying fire-control radars on enemy surface warships. Radar jamming devices also began appearing on late-war US Navy submarines.

Sonar

During the war in the Pacific US Navy fleet-type submarines had both a passive and active sonar system. Passive sonar uses underwater microphones to 'listen' for sounds.

Active sonar sends a pulse of energy (a 'ping') that reflects off objects, identifying their location and distance. From a US Navy manual comes the following passage:

> As a sonar operator, you will have a most important job. On a patrol in enemy waters the lives of your shipmates may be in your hands. You must know your gear and what it can do. You must be able to recognize and interpret the sounds that you hear. You must be able to operate the controls the way you drive a car – automatically without thinking.

A submarine sonar system that appeared just before the war in the Pacific had been assigned the designation 'WCA'. It could be employed in both the passive and active roles and also perform echo-ranging and depth-sounding. Unfortunately, while the active portion of the device worked reasonably well, the passive sonar portion did not. The 1941 version had the designation WCA-1 and a 1943 model WCA-2.

A passive-only sonar system that appeared on US Navy submarines in 1943 bore the designation 'JP'. The biggest drawback with JP is that it could only be employed successfully when a submarine ran at low speed. The passive JP sonar system was in turn replaced by a much-improved and more capable version labelled the 'JT' in 1945.

The WCA and the JT sonar systems were both to be replaced by a new sonar system labelled the 'WFA' that went onto a single *Tench*-class submarine named the *Conger* (SS-477) commissioned in February 1945. However, that submarine arrived too late in the Pacific to see action.

Before the Second World War, the US Navy had over-estimated the effectiveness of ASW vessels and their depth-charges. This lead to a doctrine that called for US Navy submarines to make their final approach to enemy ships submerged, using only sonar to guide their torpedo attacks, rather than at periscope depth or on the surface.

Early-war patrols by US Navy submarines met with very little success using the sonar attack technique. The eventual solution involved replacing the pre-war submarine commanders with a new group of far younger and more aggressive officers willing to do whatever it took to sink enemy ships.

Other Electronic Devices

Found on wartime US Navy submarines in the radio room (adjacent to the control room) would have been the Electric Cipher Machine (ECM) Mk. 2. The device, which looked like an oversized electric typewriter, was an electro-mechanical rotor-wheel cipher machine that could receive as well as send enciphered radio messages.

Originally developed by a US Army cryptologist in the mid-1930s, the design was refined by US Navy cryptologists with the help of the Teletype Corporation. The finished product that appeared in August 1941 so impressed the US Army it decided to adopt the system for itself. By 1943, approximately 10,000 were in service. The ECM Mk. 2 lasted in US Navy service until 1957.

The Japanese never managed to crack the US Navy ECM Mk. 2 codes. By way of contrast, the US Navy originally broke the Japanese Navy codes in the mid-1920s and then again in 1940 when they introduced a new system they referred to as 'Purple'.

The US Navy initially referred to the Japanese coded messages as 'Magic' and later by the British term of 'Ultra'. Information provided by Ultra to US Navy submarines acted as a force multiplier by alerting them to the location of Japanese merchant ships as well as their warships, including submarines.

There was also a Bathythermograph (BT) for detecting thermoclines, cold water layers under which a submarine could submerge to deflect enemy active sonar and make the boat more challenging to detect by enemy ASW vessels. Also, there would be an Identification, Friend or Foe (IFF) radar in late 1943, as well as a surface navigation system known as 'LORAN', short for long-range navigation.

Surface Weaponry

Besides accounting for a large number of Japanese surface ships of 1,000 tons and higher with their torpedoes, US Navy submarines also destroyed a large number of smaller Japanese vessels primarily by surface fire from their deck guns. By late 1944, when the majority of the larger Japanese merchant vessels and warships had already gone to the bottom, this became a priority.

Before the Second World War, and during the early years of the war in the Pacific, the US Navy's standard deck gun on submarines had a bore of 3in and was placed behind the fairwater. On US Navy warships, the 3in guns served primarily in the anti-aircraft role.

During the first few months of the war in the Pacific, US Navy submarine captains had permission to move their 3in gun forward of the fairwater when in port for a refit. The interwar S-class submarines had a 4in gun fitted, some of which later showed up on wartime-built fleet submarines as a replacement for their 3in guns.

The exception to 3in guns on US Navy fleet submarines involved the pre-war built and commissioned V-4 through to V-6 submarines. They had at one point two 6in guns, one located behind the fairwater and another forward of it. These guns were the largest ever fitted to a US Navy submarine.

By the latter part of the Second World War, the standard deck gun on US Navy submarines was a 5in 25-calibre. They would prove their worth over and over again. In an extract from a government publication titled *US Bureau of Ordnance in World War II* appears a passage extolling the wartime effectiveness of the 5in deck guns:

Deck guns [5in] gave a good account of themselves during the war. Nineteen large ships aggregating 86,000 tons and hundreds of smaller craft, which more than equaled this total, were sunk by accurate shellfire. This was indeed an excellent return from a modest investment which did not exceed $12,000.00. The excellent reputation of the gun was still further enhanced when, late in the war, VT-fuzed [proximity] ammunition made it possible for submarine gunners to annihilate gun crews and bridge personnel on the small boats defending the Japanese mainland.

Besides the large-calibre deck gun that armed US Navy submarines before and during the Second World War, a variety of smaller-calibre weapons made their appearance: .30 calibre and .50 calibre machine guns were eventually supplemented by single-and later dual-mount 20mm anti-aircraft guns.

In turn, the 20mm guns soon were supplemented or replaced by the addition of one or two 40mm gun mounts beginning in mid-1944. Despite their classification as anti-aircraft guns, the 20mm and 40mm guns served primarily as weapons to sink small Japanese water craft late in the war. The submarine's best defence against aerial attacks in the Second World War involved submerging as quickly as possible.

Summary

Comprising only 2 per cent of US Navy forces engaged in combat during the Second World War, their submarines sank 1,178 Japanese merchant ships and 214 Japanese naval vessels, totaling 55 per cent of all Japanese ships sunk in the conflict. It took 14,748 torpedoes from 288 US Navy submarines to achieve these results.

US Navy wartime submarine losses totalled fifty-two, an 18 per cent loss rate that proved higher than any other type of US Navy warship. Of those lost, forty-one found themselves attributed to enemy action. From a post-war US Navy report dated 1949 that evaluated wartime submarine losses appears the following passage:

> Assessment of the various sources of information enumerated in Appendix II of this report results in the following estimate: twenty-one submarines, probably or possibly sunk by depth charge and/or bomb attack; five probably or possibly sunk by mines; two possibly sunk by gunfire; one probably sunk by gunfire after being forced to the surface by depth charge attack; one probably destroyed, while surfaced, by Japanese torpedo attack; and six submarines whose loss remains in the unknown category.

Of the eleven US Navy submarines lost to other than enemy action, two involved friendly-fire incidents, with another two destroyed by their own torpedoes which ran in a circular pattern; this included Commander Richard O'Kane's *Tang* (SS-306). The remaining US Navy submarines lost to other than enemy actions resulted from strandings.

Out of the 16,500 US Navy personnel that went to sea in submarines during the Second World War in a total of 1,682 patrols that could last as long as 75 days, the manpower cost turned out to be 374 officers and 3,131 enlisted personnel, which translates to a 22 per cent loss rate – higher than any other branch of the US Navy.

Shown here is *Seawolf* (SS-197), the fourth submarine in the *Seadragon* class of four boats. All were commissioned following the official beginning of the Second World War on 1 September 1939. Electric Boat built two and Portsmouth Naval Yard the other two. Almost identical to the preceding *Sargo* class, they featured a different propulsion system. (*US Navy*)

Pictured here is *Tambor* (SS-198), the first of twelve examples of the *Tambor*-class boats, all commissioned between June 1940 and May 1941. They proved to be the first fleet-type boats to have six bow torpedo tubes and provision for mounting 5in deck guns. Like the previous *Seawolf* class, the *Tambor* class had a test depth of 250ft. (*US Navy*)

(**Opposite, above**) Here the artist has portrayed the fairwater and bridge of the *Mackerel* (SS-204), one of two small non-fleet-type submarines built during the early part of the Second World War. The other submarine in the *Mackerel* class bore the name *Marlin* (SS-205). Considered a design dead-end, neither would see combat. Instead they saw service only as training boats. (*US Navy*)

(**Above**) Shown under construction is the *Grunion* (SS-216), one of seventy-seven wartime-built Gato-class submarines. Its fairwater or superstructure has yet to be fitted. The US Navy reported the submarine lost with all hands around 30 July 1942, for unknown reasons. Found in October 2008, underwater research concluded that one of its own torpedoes might have circled back and destroyed the submarine. (*US Navy*)

(**Opposite, below**) The launching of a *Gato*-class submarine named the *Scorpion* (SS-278) on 20 July 1942. Note the large pre-war-designed fairwater/bridge fitted to the submarine. The wartime censor has blocked out some of the background structures. *Scorpion* never returned from its fourth war patrol. The presumption is that it struck a Japanese underwater mine and sank. (*US Navy*)

(**Above**) Pictured here is the stern of the *Gato* (SS-212). Descended from the *Tambor*-class submarines, the *Gato*-class boats were 4ft 6in longer and displaced an additional 51 tons. The submarine's designers came to the conclusion that the pressure hull of the *Gato* class as built was capable of a test depth of 300ft rather than the 250ft test depth of the previous fleet-type submarines going back to the two boats of the *Cachalot* class. (*US Navy*)

(**Opposite, above**) The early-production *Balao*-class submarines resembled the *Gato*-class submarines coming out of modernized mid-war refits. Most of the differences were internal. An important design feature that appeared on the *Balao* class was the replacement of mild steel in the construction of the inner pressure hull with thicker high-tensile steel. This increased test depth to 400ft – 150ft deeper than the Japanese Navy thought possible – and was a tremendous advantage in evading depth-charge attacks. (*Paul and Loren Hannah*)

(**Opposite, below**) The last of the wartime-designed and built fleet boats were the *Tench* class. The example pictured here is the *Corsair* (SS-435). Laid down on 1 March 1945, the US Navy did not commission it until November 1946. Outwardly identical to the previous *Balao*-class submarines, the major differences in *Tench*-class boats were internal. Only eleven of the *Tench*-class submarines undertook war patrols, with none lost. (*US Navy*)

(**Opposite, above**) A close-up view of the large fairwater/bridge that appeared on the pre-war and early wartime-built fleet submarines. Its design had first appeared on the V-4 (SS-166), later assigned the name *Argonaut*. In this photograph, it appears on the *Trout* (SS-202) belonging to the *Tambor* class. Note the enclosed periscope housing. (*US Navy*)

(**Opposite, below**) In this picture we see the very elaborate enclosed bridge of a *Sargo*-class submarine that also appeared on follow-on fleet-type submarine classes through to the early-production *Gato*-class boats. Early wartime experience showed that they proved too noticeable to enemy observers due to their size. (*US Navy*)

(**Above**) Another design issue that came to the forefront after some of the early war patrols in the Pacific related to the metal enclosure around the periscope shears of the fleet-type submarines. They had proved too visible to enemy observation and also trapped air, slowing a submarine's descent during a crash dive and leading to their elimination as shown in this picture of the *Gato* (SS-212). (*US Navy*)

(**Above**) In this picture of an early-production *Gato*-class submarine, you can see that the metal enclosure around the aft platform deck (nicknamed the cigarette deck) of the fairwater/bridge has been cut away. There is now a mount fitted for a 20mm anti-aircraft gun. Note the extreme length of the rear portion of the fairwater, typical of early-war fleet boats. (*US Navy*)

(**Opposite, above**) In this picture, we see the *Cero* (SS-225), an early-production *Gato*-class submarine. Most of the original enclosed fairwater/bridge is gone. However, a portion of its roof remained and acted as a platform for the lookouts. A cigarette deck has now appeared on the forward portion of the fairwater/bridge for mounting an anti-aircraft gun, becoming a standard feature on the *Gato/Balao/Tench* submarines. (*US Navy*)

(**Opposite, below**) Another view of the cut-down fairwater/bridge of an early production *Gato*-class submarine, in this case the *Bashaw* (SS-241) built by General Electric. The US Navy commissioned the boat in October 1943. It performed six war patrols and accounted for three enemy ships and several smaller vessels. (*US Navy*)

The Manitowoc Shipbuilding Company built the *Redfin* (SS-273) of the *Gato* class seen here from blueprints supplied by Electric Boat. Interesting visual detail is the faired-out bottom portion of the fairwater/bridge, a design feature not seen on the *Gato*-class submarines built in naval shipyards. *(US Navy)*

The submarine officer seen here on the bridge of a fleet-type submarine has his right hand on top of a loudspeaker, nicknamed the 'squawk box'. With it, he can transmit verbal orders to the entire boat or just certain areas within. Directly below is a circular switchbox for an intercom system. Below that is the diving alarm switch. (*US Navy*)

(**Above**) Sailors of the *Balao*-class submarine *Batfish* (SS-310) built at Portsmouth Naval Shipyard are seen here attaching victory pennants to their boat's two periscope shears. Early-production *Balao*-class submarines constructed by US Navy yards like Portsmouth have a simplified periscope shear arrangement connected by horizontal support beams. Attached to the rear of the periscope shears are two connected masts for mounting radar antennas. (*US Navy*)

(**Opposite, above**) In this image we see the fairwater/bridge of the early-production *Balao*-class submarine *Hardhead* (SS-365) built by Manitowoc Shipbuilding Company to Electric Boat's design. Note that the supporting framework connecting the two large periscope shears is of a different design to that of the early-production *Balao*-class submarines built by US Navy yards. (*US Navy*)

(**Opposite, below**) A view of the *Clamagore* (SS-343), an early-production *Balao*-class submarine built by Manitowoc Shipbuilding Company, shows the bridge arrangement of the boat's fairwater. It features a 40mm anti-aircraft gun on either side of the fairwater/bridge, a late-war feature. Commissioned in June 1945, it arrived too late to see combat during the Second World War. (*US Navy*)

(**Above**) Appearing on late-production *Balao*-class submarines such as the *Pampanito* (SS-383) seen here and the follow-on *Tench*-class submarines was a revised arrangement of periscope shears and masts. Attached to the rear periscope shear is a mast mounting the paraboloid antenna of an SJ radar. Provided with its shear at the rear of the fairwater/bridge is the paraboloid antenna of an SV radar. (*Paul and Loren Hannah*)

(**Opposite, above**) Due to the constant changes made to *Gato*- and *Balao*-class submarines during the Second World War, their silhouettes and deck gun arrangement varied greatly. Pictured here is the *Gato*-class submarine *Cod* (SS-224) in its late-war appearance, with two 40mm anti-aircraft guns and a separate shear at the rear of the fairwater/bridge for mounting a whip antenna. (*Paul and Loren Hannah*)

(**Opposite, below**) Not only were wartime *Gato*-class submarines' fairwaters/bridges modified to reduce their silhouette, but many of the pre-war fleet boats also went through the same process. In this 1946 picture we see the *Searaven* (SS-196), a pre-war *Sargo*-class submarine, with a late-war *Gato*-class fairwater/bridge arrangement. (*US Navy*)

CONNING TOWER
USS PARCHE (SS-384)
COMMISSIONED 1943
STRICKEN 1969

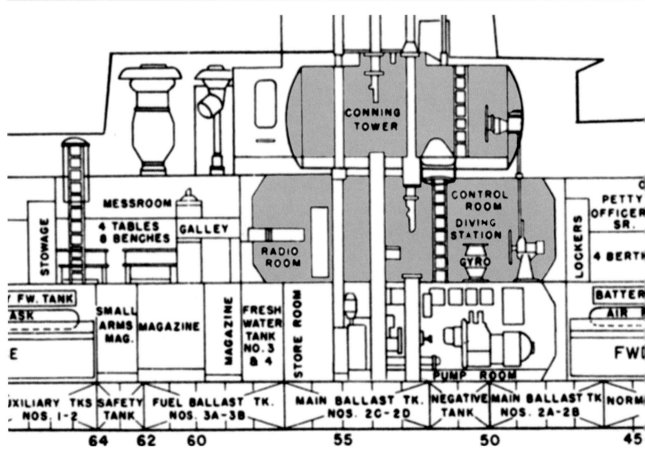

CONNING
TOWER

CONTROL
ROOM

DIVING
STATION

GYRO

PETTY
OFFICER
SR.

4 BERTH

LOCKERS

STOWAGE

MESSROOM

4 TABLES
8 BENCHES

GALLEY

RADIO
ROOM

FW. TANK

ASK

E

SMALL
ARMS
MAG.

MAGAZINE

MAGAZINE

FRESH
WATER
TANK
NO. 3
& 4

STORE ROOM

BATTER

AIR

FWD

PUMP ROOM

XILIARY TKS
NOS. 1-2

SAFETY
TANK

FUEL BALLAST TK.
NOS. 3A-3B

MAIN BALLAST TK.
NOS. 2C-2D

NEGATIVE
TANK

MAIN BALLAST TK.
NOS. 2A-2B

NORM

64   62   60   55   50   45

(**Left**) An artist's representation of the conning tower within a fleet-type submarine during the Second World War. The submarine's two periscopes could be raised and lowered from the bottom of the boat's inner watertight pressure hull via cables for viewing from the conning tower or the control room which was located directly below.

(**Right**) Despite the advent of a variety of electronic sensors such as radar and sonar on wartime US Navy fleet-type submarines, human lookouts remained an important asset on such vessels throughout the war in the Pacific. In this artist's portrayal we see the lookouts scrambling through a submarine's conning station to reach their stations on the fairwater/bridge. (*US Navy*)

(**Opposite, above**) Inside the non-watertight fairwaters of all US Navy fleet-type submarines were watertight horizontal cylinders referred to as 'conning towers', as pictured here. Some 14ft long with a width of 8ft, they were the attack centres of the boats. The first horizontal conning tower appeared on the V-4 (SS-166) named the *Argonaut*. Previous US Navy submarine conning towers were vertical. (*Paul and Loren Hannah*)

(**Opposite, below**) From a US Navy manual comes this line illustration of a *Balao*-class submarine which shows the location of the control room in the boat's hull and the conning tower above it in the fairwater. The working arrangement between the men in the conning tower and control room during combat appears in the classic 1958 Hollywood submarine movie *Run Silent, Run Deep* starring Clark Gable and Burt Lancaster. (*US Navy*)

(**Opposite, above**) Inside the *Cod* (SS-224), a *Gato*-class submarine, we see the ladder leading up from the control room to the conning tower. Both of the submarine's periscopes are visible. Other devices located in the conning tower would be a radio direction-finder, a gyro repeater and pressure gauges. (*Paul and Loren Hannah*)

(**Opposite, below**) Pictured here are the two periscopes of submarine V-5 (SS-167) named the *Narwhal*. The forward periscope is always referred to as No. 1 and the periscope behind it as No. 2. On early-production *Gato*-class submarines, their No. 1 periscope was labelled the 'attack periscope' or 'needle periscope' as it had a minimum diameter head to minimize its 'feather' (how much the water's surface was disturbed), as well as the visibility of the periscope itself. (*US Navy*)

(**Above**) The problem created by the feather and wake of a submarine's periscope and upper portion of its fairwater during daylight is evident in this photograph of the *Pike* (SS-173), a member of the *Porpoise* class of submarines. US Navy manuals recommended that submarine commanders expose their periscopes only when running at the slowest possible speed to reduce the wake. (*US Navy*)

The submarine commanding officer is looking into one of his two periscopes. At the top of the periscope is a scale employed to determine the target's bearing (direction). Visible at the bottom of the periscope on both sides are stadimeter dials. The officer to the right, helping his commanding officer develop a firing solution, is holding a slide rule to calculate the 'AOB' (angle on the bow, or target angle). (US Navy)

In this image we see the moment of impact when a torpedo from *Puffer* (SS-268), a *Gato*-class submarine, strikes a Japanese ship. Besides the small diameter head attack periscope, the *Gato* class originally had a large diameter search periscope with a wide-angle view. Like the attack periscope, it could be elevated to observe the sky around the submarine. (US Navy)

The importance of selecting the right men on submarines as lookouts appears in this passage from a US Navy manual: 'Every effort shall be made to pick the best men possible for this duty, and their training shall be carefully supervised … All bridge personnel shall be tested for night vision and none showing unsatisfactory night vision shall be so employed.' (*US Navy*)

There were hatches on top of both the forward and aft torpedo compartments for loading torpedoes. To assist in stowing the 16ft-long, 2,215lb Mk. 10 and the 20ft-long 3,209lb Mk. 14 torpedoes the crew erected a metal slide with wooden slats as pictured on the *Gato*-class submarine *Silverside* (SS-263). *(Paul and Loren Hannah)*

(**Opposite, above**) In this artwork we see a US Navy submarine returning to confirm the sinking of the enemy ship it had engaged during a war patrol. US Navy submarines conducted 1,474 war patrols in the Pacific. Patrols varied from 35 days' to 60 days' duration with an average of 50 days. Firing all torpedoes during the initial stages of a patrol or suffering serious damage from enemy ASW attacks could prematurely end a patrol. *(US Navy)*

(**Opposite, below**) This painting shows a torpedo coming on board an early-production *Gato*-class submarine. US Navy submarines entered into combat following Pearl Harbor with Mk. 10 torpedoes that could run at 36 knots to 3,500 yards and the Mk. 14 torpedo that could run at either 31 knots or 46 knots up to 9,000 yards. *(US Navy)*

(**Above**) Visible in the very foreground of this picture is the after escape and rescue hatch for the aft torpedo compartment on the *Cod* (SS-224). In the background is the closed aft torpedo loading hatch. To its left, the yellow-painted object is the submarine's aft emergency locator buoy. The bow emergency locator buoy is flush with the bow superstructure deck and hence not visible. (*Paul and Loren Hannah*)

(**Opposite, above**) On the *Gato*-class submarine *Cobia* (SS-245), looking up from the forward torpedo compartment we see the long ladder that leads to the closed forward escape and rescue hatch. The men that served on submarines were all volunteers. Reflecting the dangers of such service, enlisted submarine personnel received $100.00 a month rather than the $50.00 paid to those serving ashore or on surface ships. (*Paul and Loren Hannah*)

(**Opposite, below**) Visible is the forward torpedo compartment, or room, of the *Cobia* (SS-245), a *Gato*-class submarine. Clearly visible are four of the six bow torpedo breech doors. The two remaining torpedo breech doors are below the platform deck, so are a bit harder to see. The crew had to remove some of the platform deck panels to load torpedoes in the bottom tubes. (*Paul and Loren Hannah*)

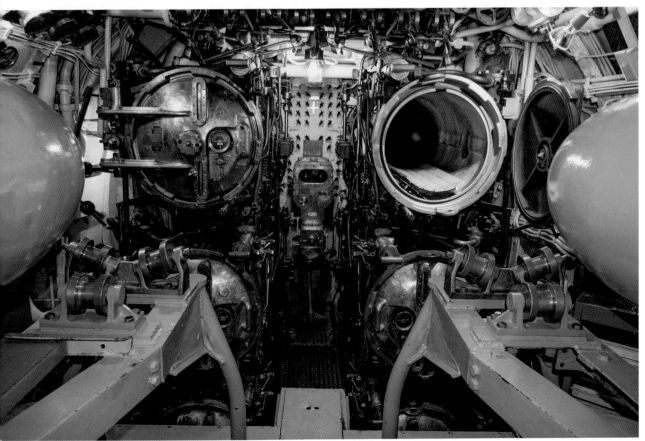

(**Opposite, above**) On display here is a submarine's 21in torpedo tube barrel. The tube was built from three bronze castings, referred to as the breech, middle and muzzle sections. The sections were cold-riveted together to form a continuous cylinder, with the joints sealed with solder. On the bottom of the torpedo barrel were four rollers to ease a torpedo into the barrel. (*Paul and Loren Hannah*)

(**Opposite, below**) In this painting we see a group of torpedomen passing their free time playing cards. The forward and aft torpedo rooms on *Gato*-, *Balao*- and *Tench*-class submarines had berthing space for approximately fifteen men each. However, some of these bunks were not usable until a certain number of torpedoes had been fired. (*US Navy*)

(**Above**) The steam-turbine-powered Mk. 14 torpedo pictured here had a warhead of approximately 500lb of TNT, later replaced by 668lb of Torpex. After exiting a torpedo tube, the arming mechanism required 450 yards' travel before arming. Serious design flaws with the torpedo's depth-keeping and Mk. 6 exploder greatly hindered its performance until late 1943. (*Paul and Loren Hannah*)

In the upper picture, we can see the closed bow torpedo shutters of the *Tambor*-class submarine *Grayling* (SS-209). The image below shows the torpedo shutters doors in their open positions, having folded inward, thereby exposing the muzzle doors of the torpedo tubes before firing. The torpedo tubes' inner breech doors are connected to the muzzle doors by an interlocking mechanism that makes it impossible to have both open at the same time. *(US Navy)*

An artist has painted a view of the aft torpedo room on a *Gato*-class submarine during a training exercise, as indicated by the casual posture of the majority of personnel present. Note the overhead chains and pulleys that were used by the sailors to move the heavy torpedoes off storage racks into the torpedo tubes. *(US Navy)*

To aid its submarines when attacking enemy surface ASW ships, the US Navy developed a small homing torpedo designated the Mk. 18. Equipped with a hydrophone (passive sonar), it could be launched from as deep as 150ft or more and find its way to the loudest noise in the immediate area, be it an enemy surface ship or submarine. It arrived very late in the war and hence saw limited use. *(Paul and Loren Hannah)*

(**Above**) In this image of the *Balao*-class submarine *Trepang* (SS-412) its four stern torpedo tubes are visible. During the war in the Pacific, US Navy submarines sank 1,113 merchant ships with another 65 probables. They also sent 201 Japanese naval ships to the bottom with another 13 probables. Included in that number were 4 aircraft carriers, a battleship and 23 submarines. (*US Navy*)

(**Opposite, above**) Greatly increasing the possibility of a US Navy submarine torpedoing its target during the Second World War was the Torpedo Data Computer (TDC), an analogue (mechanical) computer. The TDC automatically tracked the target and computed a firing solution. An example is seen here on the left-hand side of the conning room of the *Balao*-class *Parche* (SS-384). (*Paul and Loren Hannah*)

(**Opposite, below**) The inputs necessary for the TDC to compute a firing solution came from a variety of onboard sources. When running on the surface, there was the Target Bearing Transmitter (TBT) seen here on the cigarette deck of a *Gato*-class submarine to the left of the 40mm anti-aircraft gun. (*Paul and Loren Hannah*)

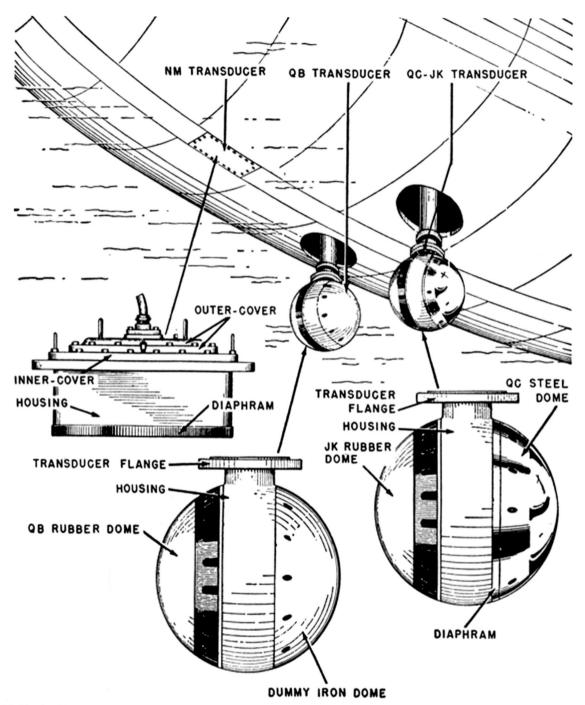

NM TRANSDUCER   QB TRANSDUCER   QC-JK TRANSDUCER

OUTER-COVER

INNER-COVER
HOUSING   DIAPHRAM

TRANSDUCER FLANGE

HOUSING

QB RUBBER DOME

TRANSDUCER
FLANGE

HOUSING

JK RUBBER
DOME

QC STEEL
DOME

DIAPHRAM

DUMMY IRON DOME

Visible in this line illustration from a US Navy manual is the retractable spherical hydrophones (referred to as projectors) of a WCA sonar unit intended to detect supersonic noises under the submarine's bow. When a target is detected, the echo-ranging sonar is trained to the target bearing and a single short 'ping' is emitted to determine range. *(US Navy)*

114

The retractable pairs of spherical hydrophones of a WCA sonar unit originally mounted under submarines' bows proved damage-prone and therefore were eventually replaced by a single non-retractable projector. The WCA sonar could operate in both active and passive modes. *(US Navy)*

On the forward superstructure deck of *Gato*-class submarine *Silversides* (SS-236) is seen the JP hydrophone (sonar) head intended to detect sonic noises. It began appearing on US Navy fleet-type submarines in 1943. By the middle of 1945, a much more capable passive sonar system designated the JT began appearing on US Navy submarines. *(Paul and Loren Hannah)*

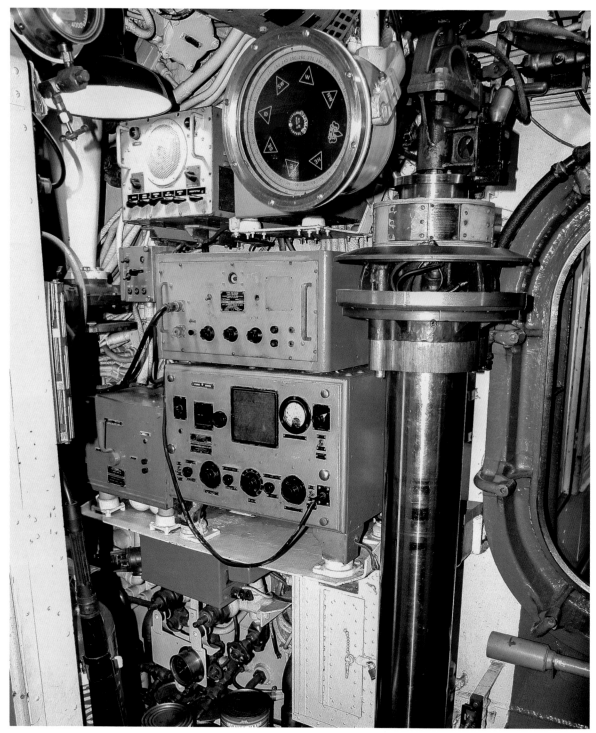

Inside the forward torpedo room of a US Navy submarine we see the receiver-amplifier for either an exterior WCA sonar projector or the exterior T-shaped antenna of the JP sonar unit. Both sonar heads were mounted on shafts that could be turned manually or power-operated from a submarine's conning tower. *(Paul and Loren Hannah)*

INDICATOR

In this picture we are looking into a *Balao*-class submarine conning tower. On the far right is the WCA stack that houses all a submarine's supersonic sonar detection. Sonic sounds travel further in water than supersonic sounds so that sonic-range sonar can detect targets at greater distances. Supersonic sonar, on the other hand, can detect the high-frequency sounds emitted by enemy ASW vessels' own active (search-mode) sonar. (*US Navy*)

(**Above**) The standard prewar armament for US Navy fleet-type submarines was .30 calibre and .50 calibre machine guns. Too short-ranged to be effective, they were replaced by single-barrel 20mm anti-aircraft guns mounted on the submarines' fairwater or superstructure decks. Late in the Pacific War, some US Navy submarines had twin-mount 20mm anti-aircraft guns installed, as pictured here. (*Paul and Loren Hannah*)

(**Opposite, above**) Most pre-war US Navy submarines following the S-class had a single 3in deck gun as seen in this picture. Besides referencing bore diameter, the US Navy also described them by barrel length in calibres (multiples of the bore size) instead of inches. Hence the 3in guns on submarines were designated 3in/.50 calibre guns. (*US Navy*)

(**Opposite, below**) The single 3in/.50 calibre deck gun's ineffectiveness on early-production *Gato*-class submarines led to their replacement by the 4in/.50 calibre deck guns removed from inactivated S-class submarines. The example pictured here is on the *Gato*-class submarine *Cobia* (SS-245) which conducted six war patrols and accounted for a total of thirteen Japanese ships. (*Paul and Loren Hannah*)

(**Above**) A wartime image of a 5in/.25 calibre deck gun crew in action. This type of gun first appeared on the *Balao*-class submarine *Spadefish* (SS-411) commissioned in March 1944. It soon became the standard deck gun for the *Gato/Balao/Tench*-class submarines, replacing the older-generation 3in and 4in deck guns during refits and new construction. Seven late-war-production *Balao*-class submarines had two of the 5in deck guns fitted. (*US Navy*)

(**Opposite, above**) The artist has painted the early-production *Gato*-class submarine *Dorado* (SS-248) firing on a derelict cargo ship for target practice during its shakedown cruise in the summer of 1943. Following its commissioning later that year, *Dorado* sailed for the Pacific from the American East Coast via the Panama Canal. However, it never arrived at the canal and it's considered possible that *Dorado* was sunk by mines planted by German U-boat *U-214* near the Atlantic entrance to the canal. (*US Navy*)

(**Opposite, below**) Seen here on the *Gato*-class submarine *Cod* (SS-204) is a 5in/.25 calibre deck gun. This particular weapon sank five Japanese ships and twenty-six smaller vessels during the Second World War. To prevent corrosion, the barrel of the gun is chrome-plated, and such weapons are referred to as 'wet mounts'. It fired a 54lb high-explosive round. (*Paul and Loren Hannah*)

(**Opposite, above**) In this image we see the support arrangement for the free-flooding superstructure located above the outer bow hull of the *Gato*-class submarine *Silversides* (SS-236). The outer hull of the submarine tapers downward, as is evident in the photograph. The actual pointed nose of the submarine is part of the superstructure, and the upper portion is referred to as the bow buoyancy tank. (*Paul and Loren Hannah*)

(**Opposite, below**) Pictured here is an artist's interpretation of the port-side bow and stern diving stations located within the control room of a fleet-type submarine. Directly above the submarine's control room is the conning tower that could be accessed by the ladder seen on the left of the painting. The two diving station operators doubled as lookouts when the submarine surfaced. (*US Navy*)

(**Above**) Located on the right-hand side of the bow and stern diving stations of a fleet-type submarine were the hull opening indicator and the various levers for the main hydraulic control system seen here monitored by the submariner pictured. Before submerging, all the lights on the hull opening indicator panel had to be green, showing that all submarine hatches and air-intake valves had closed properly. (*US Navy*)

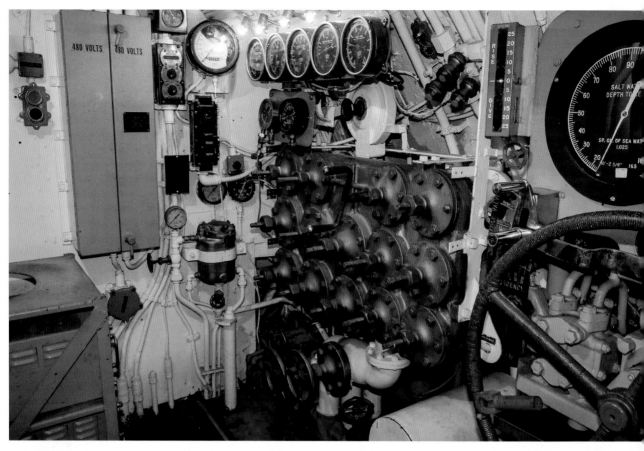

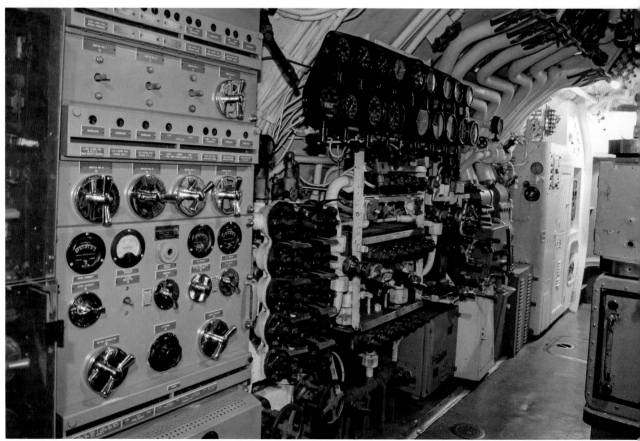

(**Opposite, above**) Visible in this image are a submarine's trim manifolds as well as trim tank gauges and trim pump controls located in the control room. A trim system is employed chiefly to maintain the boat's balance and stability. This was an important feature as submarines tend to be top-heavy, despite the fact that all their heavy machinery and storage batteries were located as low as possible within their pressure hulls. (*Paul and Loren Hannah*)

(**Opposite, below**) On the port side of the control room (opposite the bow and stern diving stations) can be seen on the left-hand side of the picture the submarine gyrocompass control board. To its right are the controls for the various air manifolds. Almost every operation in the submerging and surfacing process of a submarine is dependent on air supplied by one or more of the boat's air systems. (*Paul and Loren Hannah*)

(**Above**) The open hatch on the right side of the picture would lead to the ship's officers' living quarters. The round object in the left foreground is the master gyrocompass. In the centre of the picture is the boat's steering wheel, which turns the rudder and is operated by a helmsman/steersman. There is also a second steering wheel in the submarine's conning tower. (*Paul and Loren Hannah*)

The American counterpart of the well-known German military cipher system 'Enigma' was the electrically-powered ECM (Electric Cipher Machine) Mk. 2 seen here from a US Navy manual. It was found on the US Navy's surface warships and submarines during the Second World War. The same device when employed by the US Army had the designation SIGABA. (*US Navy*)

CODE WHEELS

INDEX WHEELS

RIBBON REVERSE LEVER

ZEROIZER

TAPE READING TAB

TAPE RELEASE TAB

CIPHER UNIT

FUSE HOLDERS

MOTOR and INDI CATOR PLUGS (See Plate 8)

CONTROLLER

RING and PAWL (See Plate 8)

COUNTER

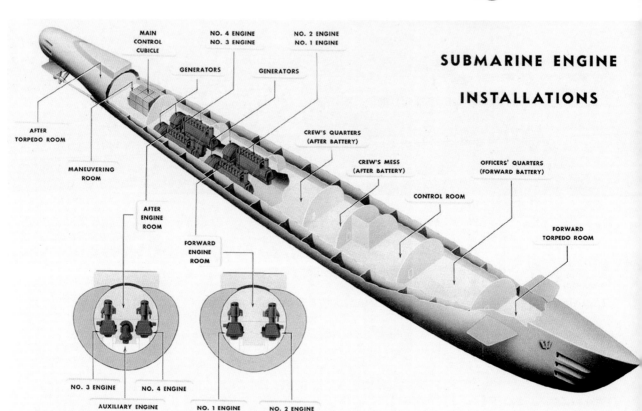

SUBMARINE ENGINE

INSTALLATIONS

MAIN CONTROL CUBICLE

NO. 4 ENGINE NO. 3 ENGINE

NO. 2 ENGINE NO. 1 ENGINE

GENERATORS

GENERATORS

AFTER TORPEDO ROOM

CREW'S QUARTERS (AFTER BATTERY)

MANEUVERING ROOM

CREW'S MESS (AFTER BATTERY)

OFFICERS' QUARTERS (FORWARD BATTERY)

AFTER ENGINE ROOM

CONTROL ROOM

FORWARD ENGINE ROOM

FORWARD TORPEDO ROOM

NO. 3 ENGINE

NO. 4 ENGINE

AUXILIARY ENGINE

NO. 1 ENGINE

NO. 2 ENGINE

The *Gato/Balao/Tench*-class submarines received power from either four Fairbanks-Morse (FM) diesel engines or four General Motors diesel engines. The engines were divided between two separate engine compartments as seen in this illustration from a US Navy manual. The engines were air-started and cooled by a combination of fresh and seawater systems. (*US Navy*)

In this picture of a model of a *Balao*-class submarine, it is possible to gain a sense of the massive size of just one of the four two-cycle General Motors main diesel engines that powered the boat. Behind each diesel engine is one of the submarine's four main electric generators that each produced 1,110kw which in turn powered four high-speed electric motors that turned the propeller shafts through reduction gears. *(Paul and Loren Hannah)*

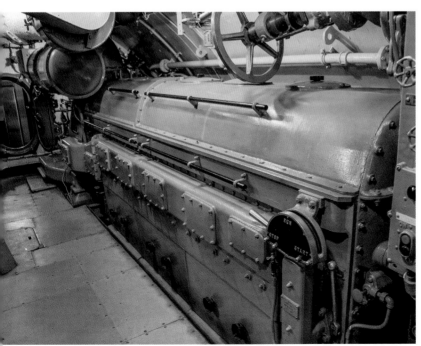

Some *Gato/Balao/*Tench-class submarines received power from Fairbanks-Morse (FM) diesel engines with an example seen here. When running on the surface, the noise within submarine engine rooms proved deafening, requiring the crews to communicate by hand signals. When the diesel engines were shut down for submerged running, the engine rooms would instantly rise to over 100 degrees due to heat build-up within the engines while running for hours. *(Paul and Loren Hannah)*

At the rear of the manoeuvring room located behind the aft engine room is the main propulsion control cubicle seen here. The electricians manning *Batfish* (SS-310), a *Balao*-class submarine, employ operating levers to perform many functions. These include starting, stopping, reversing and regulating the speed of the four main electric propulsion motors for both surface and submerged running. *(US Navy)*

With the typical wartime *Gato*- and *Balao*-class submarines having a crew complement of eighty men and operating around the clock when on patrol, the boat's galley was always a busy place. To offset the submarines' not-so-pleasant living conditions, the US Navy tried to make sure the food on board would be the best possible. *(Paul and Loren Hannah)*

(**Opposite, above**) The mess deck of a typical *Gato/Balao/Tench*-class submarine. As the mess desk could only accommodate twenty-four men at a time, the crew ate in shifts. In between meal service, the mess deck became a multi-purpose room for a variety of things such as studying, listening to the radio, playing records or writing letters home to loved ones. (*Paul and Loren Hannah*)

(**Opposite, below**) The enlisted men's main berthing area occupied a space between the crew's mess and the forward engine room and contained thirty-six bunks. Underneath the main berthing area was the aft battery compartment that contained 126 battery cells. The submarine's forward battery compartment of another 126 battery cells was under the officers' berthing area. (*Paul and Loren Hannah*)

(**Above**) The officers on US Navy submarines as on surface warships ate in their messing area referred to as the wardroom. Senior officers typically included a lieutenant commander normally referred to as the 'skipper' and his executive officer nicknamed the 'XO' who also functioned as the boat's navigation officer and was considered a future submarine commander in training. (*US Navy*)

Unheard-of on any submarine of any other navy during the Second World War was the washing machine pictured here, along with the manually-turned dryer on top. Distilling equipment provided fresh water for the washing machine as well as for other functions such as the galley, showers and for topping up the 252 battery cells on the fleet-type submarines. (Paul and Loren Hannah)

Chapter Three

Cold War Diesel-Electric Submarines

Following the end of the Second World War, the US Navy discovered that their wartime submarines were obsolete compared to the late-war German U-boats. The US Navy therefore brought back to the United States a number of German submarines including two late-war high-speed Type XXI-class German submarines for further testing and evaluation. The latter had a crew of fifty-seven, displaced 1,621 tons, had a length of 251ft 8in and a submerged top speed of 17.2 knots. Test depth was 787ft.

In the immediate post-war period, asking the American Congress to fund development of new state-of-the-art superior Type XXI U-boats was out of the question. The only feasible short-term alternative was modernization of US Navy *Gato-*, *Balao-* and *Tench*-class submarines. The goal was a submarine with operational parameters near equal to those of the German Type XXI U-boats.

The GUPPIES

In its quest to put into service submarines with upgraded capabilities, the US Navy began the 'Greater Underwater Propulsion Power' programme also known by its acronym of 'GUPPY'. Between 1946 and 1963, fifty-four examples of the *Balao-* and *Tench*-class submarines were upgraded under the GUPPY programme.

The first two GUPPY conversions, both from the *Tench*-class submarines, the *Odax* (SS-486) and the *Pomodon* (SS-486), were considered prototypes and came under the heading of 'GUPPY I'. Hull streamlining was the most noticeable external design feature of the GUPPY I submarines, including removal of the deck guns and cutting back their superstructures to reduce underwater drag and thus increase the underwater speed and range.

Instead of a steel fairwater, the two GUPPY I boats came with a streamlined fibreglass-reinforced plastic structure referred to as a 'sail'. Submerged top speed came out at 17.8 knots, with a maximum surface speed of 18.2 knots. Not wasting any time, the US Navy quickly pushed ahead with the 'GUPPY II' programme that encompassed twenty-two additional boats from the *Balao* and *Tench* classes.

The GUPPY II submarines were essentially a GUPPY I with the addition of a modified snorkel based on a wartime German design. Snorkels provided an air supply and venting of exhaust that allowed the submarines to operate their diesel engines while running at periscope depth, increasing underwater speed and range, reducing their vulnerability to enemy ASW assets and charging batteries at the same time.

The *Balao*-class submarines chosen for the GUPPY II programme had their original propulsion system, including their reduction gears, replaced by heavy-duty low-speed electric motors that had first appeared with the *Tench* class. Mounted directly on the submarines' two propeller shafts, the new propulsion system gave the GUPPY II vessels a submerged top speed of 16 knots and a surface speed of 18 knots.

Cutting Costs

The high cost of GUPPY II conversions forced the US Navy to economize. The result was ten 'GUPPY IA' conversions that were not as extensively modified as GUPPY IIs but still fitted with a snorkel. Nine *Balao*-class submarines and one *Tench*-class submarine were converted. They had a submerged top speed of 15 knots and 17 to 18 knots on the surface.

There would also be a 'GUPPY IIA' programme consisting of twelve *Balao*- and four *Tench*-class submarines. GUPPY IIAs were provided with a larger, more effective sonar room, the most significant difference from GUPPY IIs, made possible by the removal of one of the engines and rearrangement of the remaining three in each submarine. Sonar was becoming an ever more critical component of a submarine's combat effectiveness in the immediate post-war era. Maximum submerged speed was 14 to 15 knots and top surface speed 17 to 18 knots.

Fleet Snorkel Programme

As even the GUPPY IIA programme proved costlier than anticipated, between 1951 and 1952 the US Navy implemented an even simpler set of modifications for a further nineteen of its *Balao*- and *Tench*-class submarines. Labelled the 'Fleet Snorkel Programme', it was not a true conversion as had occurred with GUPPY II.

Submarines chosen for the Fleet Snorkel Programme cycled through their customarily-scheduled overhauls, and in the process acquired a few GUPPY programme design features. These included a fibreglass-reinforced plastic sail and of course a snorkel. These Fleet Snorkel Programme boats' submerged top speed came out at only 9 knots, less than their Second World War speed. Their maximum surface speed was 18 knots.

The Last GUPPIES

Due to a delay in fielding a new generation of more advanced submarines in the early 1960s and the growing obsolescence of its GUPPY submarine inventory, the US Navy established the 'GUPPY III' programme to refurbish and upgrade all twenty-four of its GUPPY II boats. However, budget restrictions led to only nine going through the GUPPY III process, also referred to as a Fleet Rehabilitation and Modernization (FRAM) programme.

Due to the ever-increasing amount of electronic equipment required on its submarines, the US Navy took the dramatic step of lengthening the GUPPY III hulls by 15ft. Within this section appeared a new sonar room. In previous GUPPY submarines, sonar equipment had been jammed into the forward torpedo compartment, reducing space available for reload torpedoes. The last GUPPY III, the *Tiru* (SS-416), left US Navy service in 1975.

Looking for a Mission

The US Navy's fleet submarines' primary mission during the Second World War was the destruction of the Japanese merchant fleet; without those ships, Japan's economy was starved of essential raw materials including oils, metals and much more. In the immediate post-war era, with the beginning of the Cold War, the threat became the Soviet Union, a land-based power, with no large merchant fleet to threaten. This left the US Navy's submarine community to consider new roles to justify its existence.

Not counting those *Balao*- and *Tench*-class submarines upgraded under type GUPPY programmes, the US Navy had almost a hundred relatively new wartime-built *Gato*-, *Balao*- and *Tench*-class submarines, including twenty-three completed after the war, that were available for conversion to fulfil a variety of roles.

Improvised Radar Pickets

One of the first new roles found for the wartime fleet boats proved to be as radar picket boats. Ten *Balao*-, *Tench*- and *Gato*-class submarines were modified under a series of programmes known as 'Migraine I, II and III'.

The US Navy had first employed makeshift radar picket boats in the closing months of the Second World War to relieve US Navy destroyers, which were taking severe losses. The submarine radar picket boats were to warn the surface fleet of incoming kamikaze attacks, submerging when they approached. They also acted as command and control vessels to direct US Navy fighters to intercept the kamikazes.

Dedicated Radar Picket Submarines

Two brand-new diesel-electric submarines of the *Sailfish* class were commissioned in 1956 as dedicated radar picket boats. They were the *Sailfish* (SSR-572) and the *Salmon* (SSR-573). At 350ft with a displacement of 2,022 tons they were the biggest US Navy submarines built until that time except for the early pre-Second World War V-boats. Unfortunately, the two *Sailfish*-class submarines lacked the submerged or surface speed to keep pace with the US Navy's aircraft carriers.

By 1961 the US Navy no longer saw a need for submarine-based radar pickets as twin-engine carrier-based aircraft such as the E1B Tracer took over that role. The two *Sailfish*-class submarines after modifications served as attack submarines until their decommissioning in 1978. The US Navy sank both boats as targets, one in 1993 and the other in 2007.

The Loon Cruise Missile

In the closing stages of the war in the Pacific, the US Navy had experimentally mounted a launcher unit for firing 5in unguided rockets on the superstructure of four of its fleet submarines. The plan called for using them in shore bombardment. Only one of the four had a chance to fire its rockets, at mainland Japan in July of 1945. The submarines had to surface to fire the rockets, necessarily putting them at risk.

Still thinking that US Navy submarines might serve a useful purpose in the shore bombardment role, the US Navy configured two of its *Balao*-class submarines, the *Carbonero* (SS-337) and the *Cusk* (SSG-348), in the post-war period to carry and fire while on the surface the subsonic 'Loon' missile, which was armed with a conventional high-explosive warhead.

The Loon was an American-built modified copy of the German wartime V-1 rocket, with a range of approximately 150 miles. Carried in a watertight container aft of a submarine's sail, it was the US Navy's first 'cruise missile'. The initial launch of a radio-controlled Loon from a US Navy submarine took place in February 1947. The Loon programme ended in 1953 as more capable cruise missiles appeared.

The Regulus Cruise Missiles

The US Navy's replacement for the Loon was the radio-controlled 'Regulus I' cruise missile. The Regulus had a range of 575 miles and was the first US Navy missile armed with a nuclear warhead. Two *Gato*-class submarines were modified to carry and fire the Regulus I missile while on the surface, the *Tunny* (SS-282) and the *Barbero* (SS-317). Like the Loon, the Regulus I found itself stowed in a deck-mounted watertight container and requiring assembly before launching from atop the submarine superstructure.

The follow-on to the modified *Gato*-class submarines was the nuclear-powered *Halibut* (SSGN-587), which featured a below-deck hangar bay capable of storing up to five Regulus I missiles. Surfacing to deploy and launch the missile on the foredeck, the *Halibut* had machinery to automate the entire process.

The first launch of the Regulus I missile from a submarine took place in July 1953. In 1956, the longer-range 'Regulus II' nuclear-armed cruise missile appeared, with a range of 1,151 miles. It employed inertial guidance instead of radio-control to reach its intended target.

Grayback Class

Commissioned in early 1958 were two newly-built diesel-electric submarines of the *Grayback* class, *Grayback* (SSG-574) and *Growler* (SSG-577), intended as Regulus II missile-launching boats. However, the Regulus II programme ended in December 1958 to provide funding for development of an intermediate-range ballistic missile launched from submerged submarines. Both the *Grayback* and the *Growler* were originally configured as fast attack submarines before selection and conversion into missile-launching boats.

With the cancellation of the Regulus II missiles, the *Grayback*-class submarines went to sea armed only with the earlier version. The two original *Gato*-class submarines armed with the Regulus I and the two *Grayback*-class submarines armed with the Regulus I would remain in service until July 1964 when the programme ended. One of the two *Grayback*-class submarines then served until 1984 as a transport boat, with the other eventually becoming a museum ship in 1989.

Hunter-Killers

To deal with Soviet attack submarines in the early Cold War period, the US Navy developed the concept of modifying *Gato*-class submarines into what became known as 'hunter-killers'. They received some of the GUPPY programme features, including a snorkel, a fibreglass-reinforced plastic sail and the heavy-duty low-speed electric motors mounted directly on the propeller shafts as first appeared on the *Tench* class.

A total of seven *Gato*-class submarines went through conversion to the hunter-killer configuration. The first example, the *Grouper* (SSK-214), was commissioned in July 1949. Reflecting their limited submerged speed, estimated to be only 9 knots, which precluded hunting Soviet submarines in the open ocean, the *Gato*-class hunter-killer submarines were to ambush their prey by hiding outside Soviet Navy bases and navigational choke-points through which Soviet Navy submarines had to transit to reach their areas of operation.

To better allow the *Gato*-class hunter-killer submarines to detect the comings and goings of Soviet Navy submarines and hide from them at the same time, they were provided with a very large and advanced passive-sonar system (based on a wartime German design) and featured an extensive array of sound-quieting features.

As a new generation of ever-faster Soviet Navy submarines entered service the US Navy's *Gato*-class hunter-killer submarines were phased out in 1959 in the ASW role. That same year, the US Navy did away with the prefix 'SSK'.

Miscellaneous Roles

Some lesser-known fleet submarine modifications in the immediate post-war period revolved around playing some role in future US Marine Corps amphibious landings. There would appear one *Balao*-class submarine configured as a cargo-carrier submarine: the *Barbero* (SSA-317). Upon the ending of the cargo-carrier submarine concept the *Barbero* became a guided missile submarine.

A single *Gato*-class submarine, the *Guavina* (SSO-362), became an oiler (floating gas station) for use during amphibious operations. When that mission failed to make much sense, the *Guavina* was eventually reassigned in 1957 to refuel seaplanes and re-designated the *Guavina* (AGSS-362). When the US Navy cancelled their seaplane programme in 1959, the *Guavina* was decommissioned and ultimately sunk as a target in June 1967.

In 1948, the US Navy went ahead with a programme to convert two *Balao*-class submarines, the *Perch* (SSP-313) and *Sealion* (SSP-315), into transport submarines. In 1966, the US Navy converted a *Gato*-class submarine, the *Tunny*, originally a guided missile submarine (SSG-282), into what became labelled an Amphibious Transport Submarine (APSS-282). The submarine had its decommissioning in June 1969.

Seven other fleet submarines found themselves confined to non-combat duties and received the classification of 'auxiliary submarines'. They performed as test platforms for a variety of electronic and design technology intended for upcoming US Navy submarine classes. By the early 1970s, all had outlived their service lives and found themselves decommissioned. Other fleet submarines would serve out their careers as static training boats until the programme ended in 1971.

The End for the Fleet Boats

As the aging submarines of the *Gato*, *Balao* and *Tench* classes were pulled from active service and replaced by newer generations of submarine classes they went in different directions: thirty-six were sunk as targets to test various US Navy weapons, while others found themselves decommissioned one last time and were stricken and sold for scrapping.

Some sixty-nine wartime fleet-class submarines went to navies of friendly countries under a variety of military aid programmes. Many of them served with foreign navies for a longer period than their service with the US Navy. A total of seventeen wartime fleet-class submarines went on to become museums in the United States.

Albacore

In the immediate post-war period, it was clear to many of those in the US Navy submarine community that the submerged speed of future submarines would be more critical than their surface speed. The German Navy and industry had concluded the same during the latter part of the Second World War and had begun testing models of tear-drop-shaped submarines in wind tunnels. However, all their efforts were for naught due to the German surrender in May 1945.

As an experimental vessel, the US Navy had a single weaponless example built of a tear-drop-shaped diesel-electric submarine named the *Albacore*. Laid down in March

1952, it obtained the designation of an 'auxiliary submarine' with the US Navy commissioning it in December 1953.

Powered by two diesel-electric engines, the *Albacore* had two counter-rotating propellers on a single shaft, in contrast to the standard submarine arrangement of two shafts each fitted with a single propeller. The latter arrangement dated back to the introduction of the US Navy's pre-First World War C-class submarines.

Underwater, the *Albacore* had a top speed of 33 knots, while surfaced it had a maximum speed of 25 knots. Having served its purpose of confirming the advantages imparted by a tear-drop-shaped hull but equipped with troublesome engines, *Albacore* was decommissioned in December 1972 and stricken in May 1980 to eventually become a museum ship.

Barracuda Class

Some in the US Navy became interested in small submarines during the immediate post-war period. Advocates thought that smaller submarines would be less costly to operate, as well as cheaper and faster to build. As many as 1,000 *Barracudas* were believed necessary to counter the perceived threat of hundreds of Soviet Navy submarines based on the German Type XXI U-boats. To build this number, many more yards would be required and a simpler design was believed to make that possible.

The small submarines of what became the *Barracuda* class proved a design dead-end as they lacked the necessary range and endurance. Thus only three examples of the *Barracuda* class were commissioned between 1951 and 1952. Originally assigned the designations K-1 to K-3, these were soon dropped and they eventually received names along with their hull classification numbers. Thus there was the *Barracuda* (SSK-550), the *Bass* (SSK-551) and the *Bonita* (SSK-552). As their role was assumed by modified wartime fleet boats as already mentioned, the *Barracuda*-class boats were decommissioned by 1959.

Tang Class

Following in the steps of the *Barracuda*-class submarines were the six boats of the *Tang* class, with the first example, the *Tang* (SS-563), laid down in April 1949 and commissioned in October 1951. The other five (SS-564 through to SS-568) were all commissioned by November 1952. Their hull shape proved to be a variation of the classic wartime fleet boat hull shape rather than the streamlined shape of the experimental *Albacore*.

Built with new high-strength steel designated HY-75, the *Tang* class had a test depth of 700ft. The class also incorporated design features from the German wartime Type XXI U-boat class. With a set of three newly-designed and compact General Motors engines, the *Tang* class had a submerged top speed of 18.3 knots, which proved faster than its surface speed of 15.5 knots. It was the first US Navy submarine to attain that goal.

As the new engines on the *Tang* class were more compact than the traditional four on wartime fleet submarines, they all fitted into a single compartment rather than the two compartments of the latter. The space-savings allowed the *Tang* class to be shorter than Second World War fleet submarines.

Unfortunately, the new generation of General Motors engines used in the first four *Tang*-class submarines did not live up to expectations. This led to their replacement by three of the wartime-developed Fairbanks-Morse engines, which in turn necessitated lengthening the submarines by 9ft to accommodate the larger engines.

The high cost of the *Tang* class and the better performance of new, faster Soviet Navy submarines eventually rendered them obsolete, resulting in their decommissioning by 1989 with most transferred to foreign navies.

Darter

Based on the design of the *Tang*-class submarines was a single example in October 1956 of a diesel-electric boat named the *Darter*, the second US Navy submarine to bear that name. Equipped with the latest electronic technology aimed at improving the US Navy's ASW capabilities, it had a surface displacement of 1,650 tons and a length of 283ft 3in.

The submerged top speed of the eighty-three-man *Darter* came out at 15.5 knots. For the installation of even more electronic equipment, the *Darter* had a 16ft extension added to its hull in 1965. The submarine remained in service until December 1989 and was eventually sunk as a target in January 1992.

Mackerel **Class**

Between 1952 and 1953, the US Navy commissioned two small diesel-electric submarines. Designated initially the T-1 and T-2, they eventually received the names *Mackerel* and *Marlin* respectively, both of which names had appeared on previous US Navy submarines.

The T-1 class submarines had a surface displacement of 339 tons and a length of 131ft 3in. Crewed by fourteen men, the top surface speed came out at 10 knots with a maximum submerged speed of 10.5 knots. The T-1 class submarines served from 1953 to 1973 as test beds for new technology and in training US Navy ASW assets. They each had a single torpedo tube. Both were decommissioned in 1973, with one eventually sunk as a target and the other donated to become a museum ship.

Barbel **Class**

The last diesel-electric submarines built for the US Navy were the three boats of the *Barbel* class. Classified as attack submarines, all were commissioned in 1959. They were the *Barbel* (SS-580), the *Blueback* (SS-581) and the *Bonefish* (SS-582). The hull design of the *Barbel* class came from the experimental tear-drop-shaped hull of the diesel-electric submarine *Albacore* laid down in March 1952.

The *Barbel*-class submarines were the first US Navy diesel-electric boats to do away with the watertight conning tower in the sail. All the command and control functions now resided in a control room below the non-watertight sail. With the combining of the conning tower functions and that of the control room within the submarine hull, the area received the label of the Control Operation Centre (COC). For surface operations, there remained an open bridge on top of the sail as on all subsequent US Navy submarines, referred to as the 'flying bridge'.

The three *Barbel*-class submarines were all decommissioned between 1988 and 1990. One of the three suffered severe damage in an onboard fire that killed twenty-four men and hence was never repaired, another became a target and the third, named the *Blueback*, became a museum. The *Blueback* also has the honour of being the last diesel-electric submarine commissioned in the US Navy in October 1959 and the last diesel-electric submarine decommissioned in October 1990.

As had occurred during the First World War, German industry in the Second World War had been on the cutting edge of submarine design; hence the US Navy acquired representative examples for testing and evaluation following the conflict. Two captured German submarines are pictured. The US Navy had also examined captured Japanese Navy submarines but was unimpressed by the designs. (*US Navy*)

(**Opposite**) A design feature that greatly improved German U-boats' survivability was the snorkel seen here fitted to the top of the raised shaft. It allowed air to be drawn in for the submarine's diesel engines and at the same time allowed their exhaust gases to be expelled. The submarine could recharge batteries and refresh its breathable air. During this time the submarine ran just under the surface, almost completely hidden from Allied ASW radar aboard aircraft and ships. (*US Navy*)

(**Above**) The most modern German Navy production submarines obtained by the US Navy following the Second World War were two Type XXI-class boats, one example of which is pictured here. Note the streamlined fairwater/bridge design that enclosed the telescopic periscope shears and snorkel shaft. Able to operate at will on the surface at night in the Pacific, the US Navy felt no urgency to develop and adopt the snorkel and took until 1948 to field an operation snorkel for its boats. (*US Navy*)

(**Opposite, above**) In this picture we see *U-3008*, a Type XXI-class German submarine operated by a US Navy crew. After an overhaul, it was subjected to operational testing by the US Navy from July 1946 to June 1948. Due to its advanced propulsion system as well as its streamlined shape, it had a submerged speed of 17.2 knots. The best the *Gato/Balao/Tench* class could muster was approximately 10 knots when submerged. (*US Navy*)

(**Opposite, below**) Unable to acquire funding in the immediate post-war era to have a new type of submarine designed and built to match or better the Type XXI-class German submarine, the US Navy came up with the 'Greater Underwater Propulsion Power' programme known as 'GUPPY'. This aimed to modernize a portion of the *Balao*- and *Tench*-class submarine inventory. Some were already in storage, as shown here in 1948. (*US Navy*)

(**Above**) The first two examples of the GUPPY class labelled the 'GUPPY I' consisted of the modernized *Odax* (SS-484) and the *Pomodon* (SS-486) seen here. Due to the haste with which they were commissioned in 1947, neither had a snorkel fitted. The aluminium sail visible proved unique to the GUPPY I programme submarines. Their maximum submerged speed came out at 18.2 knots. (*US Navy*)

(**Opposite**) As the aluminium sail designed for the GUPPY I submarines proved unsatisfactory, both Electric Boat and Portsmouth came up with somewhat similar designs for their aluminium sails intended for the 'GUPPY II' programme. Those modernized by Portsmouth such as the example pictured here had a rounded rear flair and rectangular fixed forward-facing windows in their sails. (*Paul and Loren Hannah*)

(**Right**) Those submarines modernized post-war by Electric Boat under the GUPPY II programme had a stepped sail, the rear portion of which tapered to a sharp angle as seen here. Like their Portsmouth counterparts, they had an exposed navigational bridge under which lay an enclosed bridge. The Electric Boat modernized submarines' sails had round fixed forward-facing windows. (*Paul and Loren Hannah*)

(**Below**) In response to complaints from the user community regarding the low height of the open navigational bridges on both the aluminium Portsmouth and Electric Boat sails and the amount of water cresting over them, a newer, much taller fibreglass-reinforced plastic sail seen here and referred to as the 'Northern Sail' appeared in the early 1960s as their replacement. (*Vladimir Yakubov*)

The success of the GUPPY I programme resulted in the US Navy having twenty-four of its *Balao*- and *Tench*-class submarines brought up to the GUPPY II standard between 1949 and 1951. In this picture we see the first *Balao*-class submarine, *Catfish* (SS-339), going through the upgrade. It can be identified as an Electric Boat modernized submarine by the round fixed windows located just below the open navigational bridge. (*US Navy*)

The *Diodon* (SS-349), another of the thirteen *Balao*-class submarines modernized to the GUPPY II configuration, appears in this photograph. Note that the submarine's bow no longer juts upwards as originally commissioned in March 1946. Rather, it now has a more rounded appearance. The superstructure deck has been reduced to a bare minimum to minimize underwater drag. (*US Navy*)

(**Opposite, above**) In this image, we view the *Diodon* (SS-349) on completion of its modernization into a GUPPY II submarine and fitted with an Electric Boat aluminium stepped sail. It went to sea with a maximum submerged speed of 16 knots. Unlike the GUPPY I submarines, the *Diodon*, like all the GUPPY II boats, had a snorkel fitted. Also improving the performance of all the GUPPY II submarines were more powerful storage batteries. (*US Navy*)

(**Above**) To bring down costs on the GUPPY II programme, the US Navy decided to make less extensive upgrades to twenty-six of its *Balao*- and *Tench*-class submarines. The programmes became the GUPPY IA and GUPPY IIA. On 29 May 1958, the GUPPY IIA boat the *Stickleback* (SS-415) met its end when a US Navy destroyer escort nearly cut it in half during a training exercise. (*US Navy*)

(**Opposite, below**) The small object stuck in the aluminium stepped sail of the *Volador* (SS-490), a *Tench*-class submarine modernized by Portsmouth under the GUPPY II programme (and later the GUPPY III programme), is a US Navy Mk. 44 torpedo. It found its way to that location during a 1960 training exercise in which the depth of the unarmed torpedo was entered incorrectly during a training exercise. (*US Navy*)

Another less expensive version of the GUPPY programme received the designation Guppy IB. The four submarines involved retained the same external configuration as the other GUPPY programme submarines. Pictured here is the *Icefish* (SS-367), a *Balao*-class submarine from the GUPPY IB programme, modernized with a Portsmouth aluminium stepped sail. It and its sister submarines went to friendly foreign navies under military aid programmes. *(US Navy)*

Because the *Balao*- and *Tench*-class submarines from the Fleet Snorkel Programme appeared with the same stepped aluminium sails that appeared on the early GUPPY II programme submarines, identification can be difficult. The key external difference is the retention of the original upward-pointed bow seen here with the *Torsk* (SS-423), a *Tench*-class submarine that went through the Fleet Snorkel Programme in 1952. *(Paul and Loren Hannah)*

Despite its best efforts, the US Navy could not find the funding necessary to bring all the required number of *Balao*- and *Tench*-class submarines up to any of the GUPPY configurations. To meet the minimum number of operational submarines, it came up with the least costly option possible, referred to as the 'Fleet Snorkel Programme'. Nineteen went through the process, one of which is the *Charr* (SS-328), a *Balao*-class submarine seen here with an Electric Boat aluminium stepped sail. (*US Navy*)

In this photograph, we can see the plastic Northern Sail fitted to the nine GUPPY III submarines. All nine of the GUPPY III submarines modernized between 1959 and 1963 came from the ranks of the GUPPY II vessels. The original plans had called for all twenty-four GUPPY II boats to be brought up to GUPPY III standard; however, fiscal constraints prevented that. (*Vladimir Yakubov*)

(**Opposite, above**) Pictured here is the *Pickerel* (SS-524), a *Tench*-class submarine brought up to the GUPPY III standard. All the submarines in that configuration had the plastic Northern Sail fitted. The three shark-fin-like projections on the hull are hydrophones that form part of the Passive Underwater Fire Control Feasibility System (PUFFS). To make room for additional electronics, the hulls of all the GUPPY III submarines were lengthened. (*US Navy*)

(**Opposite, below**) Besides the nine GUPPY III submarines on which it was installed, the Northern Sail eventually appeared on other modernized fleet-type boats including the *Sea Fox* (SS-402) seen here from the GUPPY IIA programme. Note that it lacks the three shark-fin-like projections of the Passive Underwater Fire Control Feasibility System (PUFFS) seen on the GUPPY III boats. (*US Navy*)

(**Opposite, above**) Between 1948 and 1953 the US Navy had ten of its wartime fleet submarines from the *Gato*, *Balao* and *Tench* classes configured as radar picket boats. These were in turn subdivided into three types referred to as the Migraine I/II/III. Pictured here is the *Requin* (SS-481), a *Tench*-class submarine that came under the Migraine III category and was the first to be converted. (*US Navy*)

(**Above**) The ten *Gato*, *Balao* and *Tench*-class submarines converted into radar pickets under the Migraine III category had their hulls lengthened by 24ft. Later conversions featured a new aluminium sail with projecting porches on either side of the navigation bridge as seen here on the *Raton* (SS-270). A *Gato*-class submarine, the *Raton* would be the last modified for the radar picket assignment. (*US Navy*)

(**Opposite, below**) Between 1956 and 1961 the US Navy employed two new-built diesel-electric submarines as dedicated radar pickets of the *Sailfish* class. With the end of the radar picket role in 1961, they were reconfigured as attack submarines as seen here with the *Sailfish* (SS-572). The submarine's Northern-type sail is much larger than the standard model as it had contained an air-search radar at one point in time. (*US Navy*)

In searching for new roles for its inventory of post-war fleet boats of the *Gato*, *Balao* and *Tench* classes, the US Navy decided that the shore bombardment role might prove productive. It therefore modified two of its *Balao*-class submarines in 1948 as an experiment, providing them with a guided missile launching ramp as pictured here on the *Carrboro* (SS-337). *(US Navy)*

The guided missile-armed *Balao*-class submarine *Cusk* (SSG-348) eventually appeared with a large watertight canister behind its sail as pictured here. It housed two guided missiles that would be assembled when surfaced for firing. Visible is a training missile referred to as the 'Loon' at the moment of launching. It carried only a high-explosive (HE) warhead and received guidance to its target by radio. (*US Navy*)

The LTV-N-2 Loon guided missile pictured here that at one point armed two of the US Navy's *Balao*-class submarines in the immediate post-war era was an American-built and modified copy of the famous German V-1 rocket nicknamed the 'buzz bomb' by the British. Primarily seen as a training weapon, the US Navy cancelled the Loon programme in 1950. (*US Navy*)

The Regulus Attack Missile (RAM) or Regulus I pictured here replaced the Loon. Armed with a nuclear warhead, like the Loon it could only be fired while surfaced. Three *Balao*-class submarines and a single *Gato*-class submarine became platforms for launching the Regulus I guided missile between 1948 and 1956. (*Paul and Loren Hannah*)

The US Navy's planned replacement for the Regulus I guided missile received the label Regulus II that appears in this image. The first submarine launch of the larger and longer-ranged guided missile took place on 18 September 1958. The US Navy's plans called for its introduction into service in 1960. Instead, the Secretary of the Navy Thomas S. Gates cancelled it in late 1958. (*Vladimir Yakubov*)

The US Navy placed two specially-designed if slightly different diesel-electric submarines into service as launching platforms for the Regulus I and II guided missiles in 1958: the *Growler* (SSG-557) and the *Grayback* (SSG-574) as pictured here. The submarines came out of the shipyards with a massive bulbous bow containing two separate watertight hangars to house the Regulus guided missiles. (*US Navy*)

Looking forward from the sail of the *Grayback* (SSG-574), we see the two separate watertight hangars that encompass most of the submarine's bow. Originally intended to be a fast attack submarine, the *Grayback* had a 50ft hull section added forward of its sail to better serve in the role of a guided missile-launching submarine. It still, however, retained six torpedo tubes in its bow and two in its stern. (*US Navy*)

The interior of one of the two separate watertight hangars on the *Growler* (SSG-557). Upon *Growler*'s commissioning in July 1957, then retired US Navy Vice Admiral Charles A. Lockwood remarked upon the potency of its nuclear-armed guided missiles by stating that they 'reduce, by comparison, the atomic bombs dropped at Hiroshima and Nagasaki to the level of 4th July firecrackers.' *(Paul and Loren Hannah)*

Launching either a Regulus I or II guided missile from the *Growler* or *Grayback* was no easy task. Everything up to firing the missiles had to be done manually, such as opening the hangar doors, placing the missile on the launching rail and unfolding its wings and tail. Then all the numerous electrical cables had to be hooked up and tested. *(Pierre-Olivier Buan)*

Inside the preserved *Growler* is shown the Regulus I missile checkout and guidance control board. Unlike the Regulus II missile that had an inertial guidance system, the older-generation Regulus I had to be radio-guided to its intended target. Once in flight, control of the missile could be handed off to an airplane or other ships or surfaced submarines. (*Paul and Loren Hannah*)

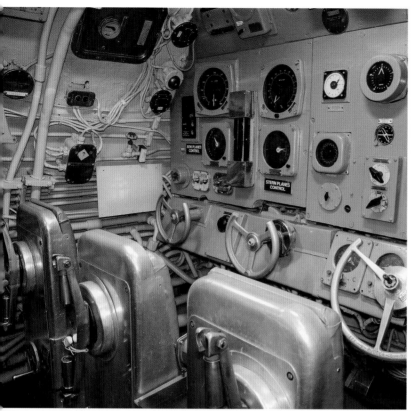

A design change arrangement within the control room of the *Grayfish*-class submarines is seen here. Unlike previous US Navy submarines that had the bow and stern diving station on the port side of their control rooms, in the *Grayfish* class they were relocated to the bow end of the control room with aircraft-type control yokes visible. (*US Navy*)

The aluminium sails that went onto the two *Grayback*-class submarines as seen here on the *Growler* (SSG-557) were very different in design from the aluminium Portsmouth and Electric Boat stepped versions. The narrowness of the sail pictured here no doubt had something to do with deflecting the exhaust blast of the rocket sleds that propelled the Regulus I guided missile off the submarines. (*Pierre-Olivier Buan*)

In April 1986, while berthed in Subic Bay in the Philippines, the *Grayback* (LPSS-574) found itself painted orange per Philippines regulations and then towed out to the South China Sea by the US Navy and sunk as a target ship on 26 April 1986. Before that time anything useful was removed for re-use on other US Navy submarines. (*US Navy*)

In this image we are looking at the front of the sail on the first of the 'hunter-killer' submarines, the *Grouper* (SSK-214) of the *Gato* class. To make room for the listening devices (hydrophones) of a new sonar system, the submarine's aluminium sail was enlarged, leading to the more rounded appearance; a sharp contrast to the standard wedge-shaped stepped sails of the other GUPPY programme submarines. (*US Navy*)

For undisclosed reasons, the US Navy proved unhappy with the sonar listening device (hydrophone) installed in the aluminium sail in the first of its hunter-killer submarines, *Grouper* (SSK-214) of the *Gato* class. This led to the other six *Gato*-class hunter-killer submarines having them relocated to an enlarged bow as seen here on the *Croaker* (SSK-246). *(Paul and Loren Hannah)*

This picture taken in August 1948 is of the *Perch* (SS-313), a *Balao*-class submarine then labelled a Submarine Transport (APSSS-313). Note the large canister behind the fairwater/bridge that stored the equipment for troops carried on board. Eventually the *Perch* was labelled an Amphibious Transport Submarine (LPSS-313). *(US Navy)*

Some Second World War fleet boats became targets during Operation CROSSROADS, a test of a nuclear bomb in July 1946 at the Bikini Atoll in the Marshall Island chain. Pictured on its return to Pearl Harbor is the badly-damaged *Skate* (SS-305), a *Balao*-class submarine. Note the posted 'Keep Clear Danger Very Radioactive' sign. (*US Navy*)

A sad fate for many wartime submarines surplus to the post-war US Navy's needs was to be sunk as a target. From the periscope of a post-war-designed and built diesel-electric submarine, we see the moment one of its torpedoes strikes the *Devilfish* (SS-292), a *Balao*-class submarine, in August 1968 off the coast of Northern California. *(US Navy)*

Supervisory naval architect Morton Gertler directs an employee in preparing a model of the planned experimental submarine *Albacore* (AGSS-569) for further tests at the David Taylor Model Basin in March 1956. The submarine's hull design came from a series of streamlined bodies developed by Mr Gertler, who supervised the testing programme that resulted in the hull and sail shape that went into the submarine *Albacore*. *(US Navy)*

The US Navy officially listed the maximum submerged speed of the experimental *Albacore* (AGSS-569), seen here at launching, at '30 knots plus'. Some have suggested the submarine's maximum submerged speed reached 50 knots. Due to its high speed, *Albacore* would be fitted with speed brakes to slow it down quickly when needed. (*Vladimir Yakubov*)

Two seamen on board the experimental *Albacore* (AGSS-569) man the engine manifold controls in one of the submarine's engine compartments. Due to the submarine's increased underwater speed and unheard-of manoeuvrability, there were hanging leather straps for standing crew members to hold on to and seat belts for those sitting at their controls. (*US Navy*)

(**Above**) In response to fears that the Soviet Navy would deploy hundreds if not thousands of clones of the German wartime Type XXI-class submarines, between 1949 and 1951 the US Navy built *Barracuda*-class diesel-electric submarines, including the one pictured here. The concept was quickly rendered obsolete by the appearance of Soviet Navy nuclear-powered submarines and no more came out of the shipyards. (*US Navy*)

(**Opposite, above**) Pictured here is the *Wahoo* (SS-565), one of six submarines in the *Tang* class, which incorporated technology from the German wartime XXI-class submarines. Commissioned in May 1952, the *Wahoo* as seen in this image has its original aluminium sail configuration that neither resembled the Portsmouth nor Electric Boat stepped sail designs of the GUPPY programmes. (*US Navy*)

(**Opposite, below**) In this photograph we see the *Tang*-class *Gudgeon* (SS-565) in its final configuration, fitted with the plastic Northern Sail that began appearing on the GUPPY III submarines in 1962. It also features the three shark-fin-like projections on the hull that form part of the Passive Underwater Fire Control Feasibility System (PUFFS). Four of the six *Tang*-class submarines eventually appeared in this configuration. (*US Navy*)

Along with the plastic Northern Sail and due to the Passive Underwater Fire Control Feasibility System (PUFFS), the four upgraded *Tang*-class submarines could fire the Mk. 45 nuclear-armed torpedo seen here. The electrically-powered weapon entered US Navy service in 1959 and remained in the inventory until 1976. *(Paul and Loren Hannah)*

Sailing along is the *Wahoo* (SS-565), one of four *Tang*-class submarines fitted with the Passive Underwater Fire Control Feasibility System (PUFFS). In total, fifty-four examples of the PUFFS went into service between 1960 and 1966 with units based on a variety of post-war-built non-nuclear and early nuclear submarines. *(US Navy)*

In dry dock here is the *Darter* (SS-576), a one-of-a-kind new-built diesel-electric submarine based on the *Tang*-class submarines. Commissioned in October 1956, the boat served in a variety of ASW training and experimental roles before being decommissioned in December 1989 after a career of thirty-three years, making it one of the longest-serving submarines in US Navy history. *(US Navy)*

One of the smallest submarine classes ever built for the US Navy were the two training boats of the *Mackerel* class between 1952 and 1953. Originally labelled the T-1 (pictured) and the T-2, they were eventually assigned the names *Mackerel* (SST-1) and *Marlin* (SST-2) respectively. During their time in service from 1953 to 1973, they generally served around Florida and in the Caribbean. *(US Navy)*

The first US Navy production submarine class to adopt the teardrop-shape of the experimental *Albacore* (AGSS-569) proved to be the three examples of the small *Barbel*-class diesel-electric boats. Pictured here is the lead ship of the class, the *Barbel* (SS-580), in dry dock. The maximum submerged speed of the *Barbel* class came out at 18.5 knots. (*US Navy*)

Chapter Four

Cold War Nuclear-Powered Submarines

The US Navy's first nuclear-powered submarine proved to be the *Nautilus* (SSN-571), the fourth US Navy vessel to carry that name. The experimental submarine authorized in 1951 received its commissioning in September 1954. The *Nautilus* had a surface displacement of 3,523 tons and a length of 320ft. Submerged top speed came out at 23 knots. It had a test depth of 700ft.

The *Nautilus* had a crew complement of 105 men. Armament consisted of bow torpedo tubes. The hull shape of the *Nautilus* proved similar to the wartime fleet submarines rather than the tear-drop hull shape of the diesel-electric *Albacore*.

As with the diesel-electric *Barbel*-class submarines, the *Nautilus* did not have a conning tower in its sail. However, sails themselves remain an important design feature as they provide underwater handling stability for submarines, a supporting structure for a variety of masts and a bridge platform when running on the surface.

In service, the *Nautilus* quickly broke all records for submerged endurance as its pressurized water-cooled nuclear reactor required no air to operate. Its duration underwater was dictated only by the amount of crew provisions. Decommissioned in March 1980, it is now a museum ship – with its nuclear reactor removed.

The Father of the Nuclear Navy

Admired by many and despised by others, the driving force behind the *Nautilus* and the introduction of nuclear-powered submarines into the US Navy was Hyman Rickover. He served nearly sixty-four years on active duty with the US Navy and was eventually promoted to admiral, making him the longest-serving officer in the Navy. He saw duty from 1929 until 1933 on S-class submarines and in the following decades rose in rank as his keen intellect became apparent to all those that served with him. As head of the US Navy's nuclear power programme in the Bureau of Ships, it was he who guided the design of the US Navy's nuclear submarines during the Cold War and it was he who selected the officers that commanded those same nuclear submarines.

Seawolf

A variation of the *Nautilus* design, the *Seawolf* (SSN-575), the third US Navy vessel to bear that name, had its commissioning in March 1957. Considered an experimental one-off submarine design, it became the US Navy's second nuclear-powered submarine. It did have bow torpedo tubes and could be called upon if required in war.

Seawolf had a liquid-sodium nuclear reactor that passed heat to the steam-plant via a liquid-sodium metal loop that used electro-magnetic pumps that had no moving parts, required no maintenance and proved very quiet. The propulsion plant was 40 per cent smaller than that on the *Nautilus* and recovered more energy per unit of fissionable material.

Unfortunately, the liquid-sodium nuclear reactor installed in *Seawolf* was considerably more expensive than the pressurized water-cooled reactor in *Nautilus*. It also suffered a serious design flaw that reduced operating efficiency and made operation riskier.

Admiral Rickover stated his reasons for losing interest in the liquid-sodium nuclear reactors as they were 'expensive to build, complex to operate, susceptible to prolonged shutdown as a result of even minor malfunctions, and difficult and time-consuming to repair.' In the end, the US Navy decided to stay with the more dependable pressurized water-cooled reactor for its submarines. *Seawolf* was decommissioned in March 1987 and eventually scrapped.

During the early period of US Navy nuclear submarine production between 1955 and 1969, the design and construction of one-off submarine designs became fairly common. Driving this practice proved to be the constantly evolving technology, forcing the US Navy to undertake a great deal of experimentation to seek out the optimum design parameters for its future nuclear submarine inventory. The funding for this costly endeavour proved relatively easy to acquire at the time due to the then frantic arms race being pursued by both the United States and the USSR.

Skate Class

Confronted by the very high cost of building *Nautilus*, the US Navy ordered a class of simpler, smaller and therefore less costly nuclear-powered submarines based on the *Nautilus* design. Labelled the *Skate* class, the four examples were the US Navy's first production nuclear-powered submarine class and classified as 'attack boats'. They retained the twin-propeller shaft arrangement of the *Nautilus* and *Seawolf*.

The eighty-four-man *Skate*-class submarines had a surface displacement of 2,290 tons and a length of 267ft 7in. Test depth was 700ft. Due to their non-streamlined hull shape, their submerged top speed came out at only 22 knots, 1 knot slower than the *Nautilus*.

The initial example of the *Skate* class (SS-578) received its commissioning in December 1957, the last in December 1959. All were decommissioned by 1986 and eventually put through the US Navy's recycling programme for nuclear-powered vessels in 1995.

Dedicated Radar Picket

In November 1959 a new nuclear-powered submarine named *Triton* (SSRN-586) was commissioned, the fifth US Navy vessel to bear that name. *Triton* displaced 6,059 tons and had a length of 447ft, making it the largest submarine ever built for the US Navy until 1981. Crew complement came out at 172 men.

Intended as the first of a new class dedicated as radar pickets, it had to match the speed of US Navy aircraft carriers. To achieve the necessary speed and provide reliability, *Triton* had two reactors instead of one as in the previous nuclear-powered US Navy submarines. The two nuclear reactors gave it a maximum submerged speed of 27 knots. With its speed and powerplant redundancy, *Triton* was assigned – and completed – the first submerged circumnavigation of the globe.

The success of early-warning airborne radar aircraft like the prop-driven Grumman E1B Tracer eliminated the radar picket role in 1961, so *Triton* took on the role of attack submarine. The much larger two-reactor powerplant was no longer necessary and never appeared on another US Navy submarine. Remaining in US Navy service until decommissioned in May 1969 and stricken in 1986, it was the first US nuclear submarine to be decommissioned and the last US Navy submarine to have a water-tight conning tower in its sail.

Skipjack Class

Previous submarine designs reflected limited submerged endurance and speed. Fleet submarines had been long and narrow; greater speeds sought after the Second World War showed this form to be unstable. Design-modelling for higher speeds trended towards shorter, wider, near-circular hulls. Thus the US Navy adapted the experimental tear-drop-shaped hull of the diesel-electric *Albacore*, yielding the design for a nuclear-powered submarine class of six attack submarines referred to as the *Skipjack* class. Both the *Skate-* and *Skipjack*-class submarines had a test depth of 700ft.

Commissioned between 1959 and 1961, the *Skipjack*-class submarines had a displacement of 3,124 tons and a length of 251ft. The hull classification number of the initial boat was SSN-585. Subsequent hull classification numbers were not in numerical sequence.

Unlike the post-war-built diesel-electric submarines and earlier nuclear-powered submarines that had double hulls, the *Skipjack* class and all the nuclear-powered submarine classes that came after it were of a single-hull design.

The ninety-three-man *Skipjack*-class submarines had a top speed of 30 knots underwater. Like the *Barbel*-class submarines, the *Skipjack*-class submarines had only a single propeller. Such a design feature ruled out stern torpedo tubes. The last example of the *Skipjack* class served until 1990. One of the class, USS *Scorpion* (SSN-589), was lost at sea sometime between May and June 1968 with all hands due to unknown causes.

From an unclassified report by the Defense Logistics Agency dated 1984 appears this passage describing the various roles assigned to US Navy attack boats:

1. Penetrate deeply into hostile seas to conduct sustained independent operations against enemy submarines and surface forces and, with the introduction of cruise missiles, to attack land targets.
2. Protect sea lines of communications.
3. Operate in direct support of carrier battle groups against both submarine and surface threats.
4. Conduct covert special missions such as mining, reconnaissance and landing of special warfare teams behind enemy lines.

Attack submarines must be effective in all ocean areas of the world including restricted waters, under the ice, in the tropics and in both deep and shallow oceans. Also must be capable of changing assignments rapidly without logistical support and be able to reposition quickly.

Halibut

Besides the various diesel-electric boats that served as launching platforms for the Loon and the Regulus, there appeared in service in January 1960 the nuclear-powered *Halibut* (SSGN-587), the second US Navy vessel to bear that name. *Halibut* had been laid down as a diesel-electric submarine, but Admiral Arleigh Burke, seeing the possibilities of missile-armed nuclear submarines, had it completed with nuclear-powered propulsion.

From 1961 to 1964, armed with Regulus I missiles, *Halibut* undertook numerous cruises in the Pacific. The introduction of Polaris-missile-equipped submarines ended the need for a cruise missile-armed submarine deterrent, so in 1965 it was re-designated an attack submarine, a role it performed until 1968.

In 1968 *Halibut* was refitted as a 'special operations' submarine capable of per-forming a variety of atypical submarine missions such as tapping underwater com-munication cables, such as Operation IVY BELLS. Decommissioned in June 1976 and struck from the US Navy's inventory in April 1986, it then went through the standard US Navy recycling programme for nuclear-powered vessels.

Tullibee

In November 1960, the US Navy commissioned the *Tullibee* (SSN-597), the second submarine to bear that name. Designed as a one-off experimental ASW submarine, it had a surface displacement of 2,640 tons and a length of 273ft, making it the smallest nuclear-powered combat submarine to ever serve with the US Navy. The maximum submerged speed came out at 14.5 knots. Eventually manned by a crew of 113, it lasted in service until June 1988, finding itself struck the same month.

The *Tullibee* featured some firsts for the US Navy's attack submarines. Instead of a large bow torpedo compartment as with all previous US Navy attack submarines, *Tullibee*'s resided amidships with the torpedo tubes on either side of the submarine's hull angled outward. This design change reflected that the entire forward portion of the submarine's bow consisted of a large enclosed spherical sonar array, a design feature on all subsequent US Navy nuclear-powered attack submarines.

New Type of Propulsion System

Tullibee also differed in that its nuclear reactor was connected to a turbo-electric propulsion system instead of the standard arrangement with a nuclear reactor con-nected to a steam turbine propulsion system. The steam turbine mechanically drove a submarine's propeller shaft(s) through a series of reduction gears. Ships' service turbine auxiliary generators convert mechanical energy into electrical power for the submarine's many electronic devices.

In a turbo-electric propulsion system the propulsion and auxiliary steam turbines are replaced with steam-driven main turbine generators as the prime movers. They convert all the available reactor power to electricity, which is sent to a common electrical bus for allocation, eliminating the reduction gears along with their associated noise, maintenance and space consumption.

The US Navy's interest in turbo-electric propulsion systems for submarines revolved around their quieter operation. This is a critical factor for attack submarines in tracking down and destroying enemy submarines should war come. Unfortunately, the available technology was not up to the task.

Narwhal

Another one-of-a-kind experimental nuclear-powered submarine ordered in July 1964 by the US Navy was the 106-man *Narwhal* (SSN-671), the third US Navy vessel to bear that name. Commissioned in July 1969, it had a surface displacement of 5,027 tons and a length of 314ft. Its submerged top speed remains classified, along with many other things including its test depth.

Intended to be the quietest US Navy submarine built up until that time, it had a natural circulation reactor that generated a lot less noise than the standard water circulating pump used in previous submarine reactors. However, a design flaw with a novel circulating water scoop could not be resolved, resulting in the idea of a natural circulation reactor coming to an end.

Some of *Narwhal*'s unique design features went into the later *Ohio*-class ballistic missile submarines. Decommissioned in July 1999, the US Navy struck it at the same

---

Identifying Code Letters

During the Second World War and Cold War era, the US Navy came up with a bewildering array of prefix code combinations to describe the various types of submarines roles. In some cases the submarine type never entered service, and some submarines had their codes changed over time as they took on new roles:

Auxiliary Submarine	AGSS
Attack (torpedo) Submarine (diesel-electric)	SS
Attack (torpedo) Submarine (nuclear)	SSN
Auxiliary Submarine (retaining attack capability)	SSAG
Ballistic Missile Submarine (nuclear)	SSBN
Bombardment Submarine (diesel-electric)	SSB
Cargo Submarine	APSS and SSA
Coastal Submarine	SSC
Communication Submarine (diesel-electric)	SSQ
Communication Submarine (nuclear)	SSQN
Electronic Reconnaissance Submarine	SSE
Guided Missile Submarine (nuclear)	SSGN
Hunter-Killer Submarine (diesel-electric)	SSK
Hunter-Killer Submarine (nuclear)	SSKN
Mine-laying Submarine	SSM or SM
Radar Picket Submarine (diesel-electric)	SSR
Radar Picket Submarine (nuclear)	SSRN
Submarine Oiler	AOSS and SSO
Target Training Submarine	SST
Transport Submarine (diesel-electric/nuclear)	APS and APSS, ASSP, LPSS, SSP

time. Despite its design differences and its experimental nature, the *Narwhal* could and did function as a fully-capable attack submarine during its service career.

Thresher/Permit Class

Even while the nuclear-powered *Skipjack* class remained on the drawing boards, the US Navy pushed ahead with its nuclear-powered successor class named the *Thresher*. Consisting of fifteen boats, the first – i.e. the *Thresher* – entered service in August 1961 and the last in 1968. One example of the class remained in service until 1996. Due to the use of stronger HY-80 steel coupled with an improved hull design, the *Thresher* class achieved a test depth of 1,300ft.

On 10 April 1963, during routine testing the *Thresher* (SSN-593) sank with all hands as well as a contingent of civilian contractors. Afterwards the US Navy did away with the *Thresher*-class name and replaced it with the new name of the *Permit* class, after the second submarine in the class. To make sure there were no more accidents as had befallen the *Thresher*, the US Navy implemented a rigorous quality control system known as the 'SubSafe Programme'.

The eighty-five-man *Permit* class was larger and longer than the *Skipjack* class due to extreme efforts aimed at quieting the submarine when submerged. It also retained the tear-drop shape of its predecessor, a hull design configuration continued on all subsequent US Navy nuclear submarine classes. Submerged top speed came out at 28 knots. Like the *Tullibee*, the *Permit* class had its torpedo compartment located at the bottom of the hull with the torpedo tubes slanted forward.

New Weaponry

Introduced into US Navy submarine service in 1956 was the Mk. 37 torpedo, a two-speed, electrically-driven acoustic homing weapon. It remained the US Navy's standard anti-submarine weapon until the early 1970s. Approximately 11ft long, the torpedo weighed 1,430lb and had a 330lb warhead. At 17 knots it had a maximum range of 23,000 yards. When set for a maximum range of 10,000 yards it had a top speed of 26 knots.

The longest-serving torpedo on US Navy submarines has been the Mk. 48 torpedo, the replacement for the Second World War Mk. 14. It entered service in 1972 and continues in use with ever-more advanced versions till today. From an online US Navy fact file appears this passage describing the latest version of the weapon:

> The MK 48 heavyweight torpedo is used by all classes of submarines as their anti-submarine warfare (ASW) and anti-surface warfare (ASUW) weapon. The MK 48 ADCAP torpedo is a heavyweight acoustic-homing torpedo with sophisticated sonar, all-digital guidance-and-control systems, digital fusing

systems, and propulsion improvements. Its digital guidance system allows for repeated upgrades to counter evolving threats through software upgrades.

Another weapon that armed the *Permit* class was the UUM-44 nuclear-armed missile known as the Submarine Launched Rocket (SUBROC). Launched from a submarine's torpedo tubes, it was the US Navy's first guided missile launched from submerged submarines, entering service in 1965. It left US Navy service in 1987.

A weapon that also first appeared on the *Permit* class and remained on US Navy submarines until 1997 was the Harpoon anti-ship missile. It is now only found on US Navy aircraft or surface ships.

Sturgeon Class

Based on a lengthened and upgraded version of the *Permit* class, there appeared in service in March 1967 the first in a class of thirty-eight submarines referred to as the *Sturgeon* class. The initial submarine in the class had the hull classification number SSN-637. Subsequent hull classification numbers were not numerically sequential. The US Navy decommissioned the last example of the *Sturgeon* class in May 2005, the *Parche* (SSN-683).

The first 28 examples of the 107-man *Sturgeon*-class submarines had a length of 292ft 3in and a surface displacement of 3,698 tons. As they had increased displacement but employed the same S5W nuclear reactors that powered the *Permit* class, they were 2 knots slower with a submerged top speed of 26 knots.

The *Sturgeon* class had a test depth of 1,300ft. The last nine examples of the class were 10ft longer than the first twenty-eight examples to provide more room for electronic equipment as well as improve the crew's living conditions.

Submarine Builders

During the 1960s there were seven shipyards, a combination of US Navy and commercial yards, building submarines. The US Navy yards included Mare Island and Portsmouth. The commercial yards included Ingalls Shipbuilding, New York Shipbuilding, Newport News Shipbuilding and two owned by Electric Boat, which had become the General Dynamics Corporation in 1952.

Over time the number of submarine builders has decreased. Mare Island constructed its last submarine in 1972, with Portsmouth building its last in 1969. Ingalls received a contract to build twelve submarines in 1957 with the last completed in 1973. In March 2011 Huntington Ingalls Industries became the owner of both Ingalls and Newport News.

New York Shipbuilding built its last submarine in 1967 and went out of business the following year. The only two shipyards now capable of building submarines are Huntington Ingalls Industries Newport News and General Dynamics Electric Boat.

Seven of the nine lengthened submarines of the *Sturgeon* class would eventually have a unique watertight hangar referred to as the Dry Deck Shelter (DDS) attached to their upper hull. Within the DDS was stored specialized US Navy SEAL equipment. The SEAL teams carried onboard the submarines could access their equipment via the middle transfer chamber within the DDS.

Tomahawk Cruise Missile

A weapon not seen on the *Permit* class but appearing on the *Sturgeon* class was the Tomahawk cruise missile that launched from the submarine's torpedo tubes. Once in the air, the Tomahawk has a cruising altitude of between 98ft and 164ft. The weapon also appears on US Navy surface ships.

Initially there were two types of Tomahawk cruise missiles launched from the *Sturgeon* class: one labelled a land-attack model and the other an anti-ship model. There is now a multi-purpose Tomahawk on newer classes of US Navy submarines that fulfils both roles known as the 'Tactical Tomahawk'. From a US Navy online fact file appears a description of the weapon:

> The Tomahawk Block IV (Tactical Tomahawk, TLAM-E), conventional variant, which entered the Fleet in 2004, adds the capability to re-programme the missile while in flight via two-way satellite communications to strike any of fifteen pre-programmed alternate targets or redirect the missile to any Global Positioning System (GPS) target coordinates.

Glenard P. Lipscomb

In spite of reliability problems with the *Tullibee*'s experimental turbo-electric propulsion system, such was the allure of quieter operation that the US Navy tried a second time to see if it could perfect it with the commissioning of the *Glenard P. Lipscomb* (SSN-685) in December 1974. Based on the general design of the *Sturgeon* class, it had a surface displacement of 5,906 tons and a length of 365ft.

Due to its increased size and displacement, the 121-man boat proved slower than the *Sturgeon* class, having a top speed of only 23 knots. The drop in the submarine's top speed and continued reliability issues caused the US Navy to lose interest in the experimental turbo-electric propulsion system. No additional nuclear-powered submarines were fitted with this propulsion system. The US Navy had the *Glenard P. Lipscomb* decommissioned in July 1990 and struck the same month.

Los Angeles Class

As the *Permit*- and *Sturgeon*-class submarines reached the end of their useful service lives and the Soviet Navy began deploying ever faster and deeper-diving nuclear-powered submarines, the US Navy had to act quickly to redress the undersea balance of power, which resulted in the sixty-two boats of the *Los Angeles* class.

The first *Los Angeles*-class submarine had its commissioning in November 1976 with the hull classification number SNN-688. Following hull classification numbers were not all in numerical sequence. As of late 2018, approximately thirty-five of the *Los Angeles*-class submarines remain in service.

The 143-man *Los Angeles*-class submarines have a length of 360ft and a displacement of 6,082 tons. To regain the submerged speed of 30 knots obtained by the *Skipjack* class, the *Los Angeles*-class submarines were built with the more powerful nuclear reactor, which in turn increased its length and beam compared to the earlier *Sturgeon*, *Skipjack* and *Permit* classes.

According to the US Navy, the *Los Angeles*-class submarines have a test depth of only 650ft and a submerged top speed of over 25 knots. However, a well-respected British-based publication on modern naval affairs suggests that their test depth is 1,475ft. Other well-thought-of sources believe the *Los Angeles*-class submarines have a maximum submerged speed of somewhere between 30 and 33 knots.

There have been design changes over the course of construction within the class. The last twenty-three examples came out of the shipyards with an arrangement of twelve vertical launch tubes armed with Tomahawk cruise missiles, fitted in their bows. These boats are known as the 'Improved Los Angeles-class submarines'. They also have additional quieting features, the ability to deliver mines and an under-ice capability that the first thirty-nine examples did not have.

Up until 1992, fifty-seven of the *Los Angeles*-class submarines had a nuclear-warhead-armed version of the Tomahawk cruise missile labelled the Tomahawk Land Attack Missile-Nuclear (TLAM-N). These remain in long-term storage to be returned to submarine service if required.

Seawolf Class

The US Navy's intended replacement for the *Los Angeles*-class attack submarines was to have been twenty-nine boats of the *Seawolf* class with design work beginning in 1983. Construction of the first example of the *Seawolf* class started in October 1989 with the hull classification number SSN-21 beginning a new hull classification sequence. From the General Dynamics Electric Boat website appears this description of the *Seawolf*-class submarines:

> … the first new top-to-bottom attack submarine design since the early 1960s – are the fastest, quietest, most heavily armed undersea vessels in the world. *Seawolf* submarines provide the US Navy with undersea weapons platforms that can operate in any scenario against any threat, with mission and growth capabilities that far exceed *Los Angeles*-class submarines.

With the ever-escalating costs of the *Seawolf*-class submarines and the end of the long-running Cold War in 1991, the US Navy completed construction of only three boats, cancelling the rest. The three boats' commissioning took place between July 1997 and February 2005. As of 2018, all three remain in active service.

The first and second examples, the *Seawolf* (SSN-21) and *Connecticut* (SSN-22), have a surface displacement of 9,137 tons and a length of 353ft. The official top submerged speed on the submarines is 25 knots plus. Respected sources report the maximum speed of the boats is 35 knots with a test depth of 1,300ft. The personnel complement is between 130 and 140. Rather than the 21in-diameter torpedo tubes dating back to the Second World War, the *Seawolf*-class submarines have 30in-diameter torpedo tubes.

Jimmy Carter

The third and final example of the *Seawolf* class, named the *Jimmy Carter* (SSN-23), had a 100ft-long section inserted into its hull. The extension bears the title of the Multi-Mission Platform (MMP). A 1999 article by US Navy Rear Admiral John P. Davis titled *USS Jimmy Carter (SSN-23): Expanding Future SSN Missions* explains the intended purpose of the MMP:

> It will support classified research, development, test and evaluation (RDT&E) efforts for notional naval special warfare (NSW) missions, tactical undersea surveillance, and undersea warfare concepts … These changes will have no direct impact on the ship's organic warfighting capability but will give the submarine an enhanced payload capability with a more modular architecture.

The *Jimmy Carter* has a surface displacement of 12,139 tons and a length of 452ft 8in. Due to its increase in size and displacement, the maximum submerged speed is no doubt less than that of the first two submarines in its class.

Intermediate-Range Ballistic Missiles

In the immediate post-war period the US Navy concentrated on surface-launched cruise missiles rather than intermediate-range ballistic missiles (IRBM) launched from submerged submarines. A senior US Navy admiral had gone as far as banning US Navy officers from even suggesting a requirement for IRBM-armed submarines between 1953 and 1955.

In November 1955, the US Navy found itself pushed against its wishes into a joint programme with the US Army to develop a liquid-propellant, Intermediate Range Ballistic Missile (IRBM) assigned the name 'Jupiter'. The US Navy felt that a liquid-propellant missile would not be safe to launch from either surface ships or submarines and therefore preferred a solid-propellant design.

Breaking with the Jupiter programme, the US Navy announced in December 1956 the development of a solid-propellant IRBM labelled the 'Polaris'. The initial designation assigned to the Polaris was Fleet Ballistic Missile (FBM). It later became known as a Submarine-Launched Ballistic Missile (SLBM).

Boomers

The Soviet launch of the world's first Intercontinental Ballistic Missile (ICBM) in August 1957 and the debut of the world's first satellite named the Sputnik in October 1957 was a serious wake-up call to the US Navy, which accelerated its efforts to field a nuclear-powered submarine armed with Polaris. Instead of designing and building from the ground up a new submarine class to carry the Polaris, the Navy decided to use a 130ft lengthened version of five *Skipjack*-class attack submarines.

The US Navy would eventually commission four additional classes of progressively larger and improved SLBM-armed nuclear-powered submarines through to 1967. In total the five classes added up to forty-one boats. As a generic name, they were referred to as the '41 for Freedom' group as they acted as a successful deterrent to Soviet aggression during the Cold War.

The 41 for Freedom group comprised five *George Washington*-class submarines, five *Ethan Allen*-class submarines, nine *Lafayette*-class submarines, ten *James Madison*-class submarines and twelve *Benjamin Franklin*-class submarines. Their hull classification numbers were not in numerical sequence. A popular US Navy nickname for all nuclear-powered ballistic missile submarines is 'Boomers'.

Crew complement on the *George Washington* class numbered 112 with larger follow-on classes having a crew of 140 men. Maximum submerged speed on all five classes ranged between 21 and 22 knots. All five classes of SLBM-armed submarines carried sixteen missiles in a large compartment behind their sail. They also retained their bow torpedo tubes. They varied in size, with the first *George Washington*-class boats having a surface displacement of 6,055 tons and a length of 381ft 6in.

The final *Benjamin Franklin*-class submarines had a surface displacement of 7,443 tons and a length of 425ft. Test depth on the *George Washington* class came out at 700ft with the four following classes having a test depth of 1,300ft. The US Navy decommissioned the last *Benjamin Franklin*-class submarine in April 2002.

Of the 41 for Freedom group submarines, eight were for a short time reclassified as attack submarines between 1980 and 1992. However, they proved badly suited to that role and went through decommissioning between 1981 and 2002. Two eventually became static training vessels. Four of the 41 for Freedom group submarines went on to become transport boats for special operation forces. The first two entered into service in 1991, with all four pulled from service by 2002.

Missile Types

There were three progressively-improved versions of the Polaris brought into service (the A1 through to A3) on the 41 for Freedom group, with the last having a range of

2,877 miles. The initial version of the Polaris had a range of only 1,611 miles. In 1970, there appeared the 'Poseidon' missile as a replacement for the Polaris. From a US Navy online site appears this extract on the weapon:

> The next generation of fleet ballistic missiles to follow Polaris was the Poseidon C-3 missile. Longer, larger and heavier than the Polaris, the C-3 carried multiple warheads, each of which could be targeted separately over a wider space and variety of target footprints. The C-3 Poseidon was twice as accurate, and its warheads had twice the explosive power of the A-3. Considering these factors, experts believe the C-3 was eight times as deadly as the A-3.

Due to the larger diameter of the Poseidon, it could not fit into the *George Washington*- or *Ethan Allen*-class submarines' launch tubes. However, the Poseidon did fit into the *Lafayette*-class submarines and its successor-classes' launch tubes. In 1979, the 'Trident I' came into service on some of the *James Madison*- and *Benjamin Franklin*-class submarines as a replacement for the Poseidon, which the US Navy retired from service in 2005.

From a Lockheed Martin online site appears this extract on the weapon:

> The Trident I C4 missiles were the longest continuously-operated Fleet Ballistic Missiles ever deployed by the US Navy. Using advanced technology in propellants and new weight-saving materials, the Trident I C4 missile incorporated the multiple independently-targeted vehicle capability of its predecessor Poseidon and provided an astounding range of more than 4,000 nautical miles [4,603 miles] with a full payload.

Ohio Class

To replace the *Benjamin Franklin*- and *Lafayette*-class ballistic missile submarines, the US Navy commissioned eighteen *Ohio*-class ballistic missile submarines between 1976 and 1997. Initially, the US Navy called for twenty-four examples. However, with the end of the Cold War, plans for construction of the last six were cancelled.

The hull classification numbers of *Ohio*-class submarines are in numerical sequence with the first in the class being SSGN-726 and the last SSBN-743. The first four *Ohio*-class submarines bore the letter prefix SSGN and the last fourteen the prefix SSBN.

The *Ohio* class is the largest submarine ever placed into service by the US Navy with a surface displacement of 16,764 tons and a length of 560ft. The crew complement is 155. The top speed and test depth are officially reported by the US Navy to be respectively 20 knots and 800ft.

Ohio *Calls Details*

The main hull penetrating periscope on the *Ohio* class is designated the Type 18. It first appeared on the *Los Angles*-class attack submarines in the 1960s. From the autumn 2004 issue of *Undersea Warfare* magazine appears the following passage describing the various features of the Type 18 Periscope:

> Important features of the Type 18 include multiple magnification levels, single-axis stabilization, digital photography, low-light image intensification, color television, and day-and-night viewing capabilities. The Type 18 periscope is currently undergoing upgrades for a video package known as SUBIS (Submarine Imaging Subsystem), a set of analogue video and digital still cameras that record the view from the periscope and provide image enhancement software for image analysis.

Besides bow torpedo tubes, the main armament of the first eight of the *Ohio* class originally consisted of twenty-four Trident I SLBMs, each with an 'MIRV' (Multiple Independently Targetable Re-entry Vehicle) containing anywhere between eight to twelve warheads. The US Navy eventually decreased the number of missiles to only twenty Trident I SLBMs on each *Ohio*-class boat and only eight MIRVs per missile to meet treaty requirements. The first launch of a Trident I from an *Ohio*-class submarine took place in January 1982.

An upgraded version of the Trident I C-4 missile, referred to as the Trident II C-5, entered service on the ninth *Ohio*-class submarine and was eventually retrofitted to four of the first eight built. The initial launch of a Trident II from an *Ohio*-class submarine took place in March 1989 and proved to be a failure. However, the second launch in August 1989 was successful. The *Ohio* class has also acquired the nickname of the 'Trident class', reflecting its main armament.

The Trident II is reported to be able to place all eight nuclear warheads of an individual MIRV within a circle of only 560ft from a range of 4,603 miles. The maximum range of all the various versions of the Trident II missile is classified, but respected sources list it as 7,500 miles. It travels to its target(s) at a speed of approximately 18,000mph.

New Roles for the Ohio Class

A study concluded in 1994 decided that following the end of the Cold War the US Navy did not require eighteen *Ohio*-class ballistic missile submarines. Therefore four became what the US Navy labelled 'Guided Missile Submarines' (SSGN) between 2002 and 2007, the main armament consisting of conventionally-armed Tomahawk cruise missiles. These four submarines are also informally referred to as the 'Tactical Trident' submarines.

A description of these four re-purposed *Ohio*-class submarines appears in this passage from an online US Navy fact file:

> Combined, the four SSGNs represent more than half of the Submarine Force's vertical launch payload capacity with each SSGN capable of carrying up to

154 Tomahawk land-attack cruise missiles. The missiles are loaded in seven-shot Multiple-All-Up-Round Canisters (MACs) in up to 22 missile tubes.

The four much-modified *Ohio*-class submarines also received a secondary mission of supporting US Navy SEALs. With this mission came the Advanced SEAL Delivery Systems (ASDS), which is in effect a small 50-ton displacement submarine. Some of their now unused vertical missile tubes in the modified *Ohio*-class submarines became stowage canisters for SEAL food and equipment. These same unused vertical missile tubes are also intended to accommodate future payloads such as new types of missiles, unmanned aerial vehicles and unmanned undersea vehicles.

In the summer of 1951, the United States Congress authorized funding for the world's first nuclear-powered submarine seen here, named the *Nautilus* (SSN-571). Modelled on the diesel-electric-powered *Tang*-class submarine, the US Navy commissioned it on 30 September 1954. The first nuclear-powered Soviet submarine, the K-3, did not go to sea until three and half years later. (*US Navy*)

(**Opposite, above**) Taken in July 1952 was this photograph of Captain (later Admiral) Hyman G. Rickover on the left and Secretary of the Navy Dan A. Kimball on the right. Both men are looking over a very stylized model of the future *Nautilus* (SSN-571). Rickover sports a medal on his jacket lapel for his efforts in shepherding the submarine's development. (*US Navy*)

(**Opposite, below**) Decommissioned in March 1980, the *Nautilus* (SSN-571) went on to see a second career as a museum ship in April 1986 at the Submarine Force Museum located at New London, Groton, Connecticut. In this picture taken in May 1985 at Mare Island Naval Shipyard, we see the *Nautilus* receiving a new paint job before going on display. (*US Navy*)

(**Above**) Another one-off experimental or prototype submarine following the *Nautilus* (SSN-571) was the *Seawolf* (SSN-575) seen here. Commissioned in March 1957, it went to sea with a liquid-sodium nuclear reactor instead of the pressurized water-cooled nuclear reactor of the *Nautilus*. Unfortunately, unforeseen design flaws quickly rendered the *Seawolf*'s liquid-sodium reactor a failure in service. (*US Navy*)

Designed as a radar picket operating ahead of carrier task forces, the *Triton* (SSRN-586) seen here had two nuclear reactors fitted rather than the standard single reactor to provide it with the sustained speed of 28 knots required for the job. When the role of submarine radar picket disappeared in 1961 with the advent of radar-equipped planes flying off aircraft carriers, it became an attack submarine. (*US Navy*)

(**Opposite, above**) In the foreground is the *Seawolf* (SSN-575) and in the background the *Nautilus* (SSN-571). The *Seawolf* has an Electric Boat stepped aluminium sail and the *Nautilus* a one-of-a-kind aluminium sail. Whereas the *Nautilus* had its sonar dome under the front of its bow, on the *Seawolf* it is mounted on the top of the submarine's bow. (*US Navy*)

(**Opposite, below**) The US Navy's first production nuclear-powered submarines were the four boats of the *Skate* class. Pictured here is the *Sargo* (SSN-583) of the *Skate* class at its launching on 10 October 1957. They were nuclear-powered copies of the six diesel-electric post-war *Tang*-class submarines. Their small size compared to the much larger *Nautilus* (SSN-571) and *Seawolf* (SSN-575) revolved around the US Navy trying to keep costs down. (*US Navy*)

Pictured here is the *Shark* (SSN-591) before launching, one of six nuclear-powered submarines of the *Skipjack* class. It was the first production US Navy nuclear-powered submarine to adopt the teardrop shape of the experimental diesel-electric-powered *Albacore* (AGSS-569). The interior arrangement of the *Skipjack* class came from the three diesel-electric-powered submarines of the *Barbel* class. (*US Navy*)

One of the defining external features of the *Skipjack* class of nuclear-powered attack submarines would be the relocation of the forward manoeuvring planes from the bow to the sail as seen here. A second important design change was the *Skipjack*-class single-screw design instead of the two screws typical of previous nuclear-powered submarines. *(US Navy)*

Another unique nuclear-powered submarine design for the US Navy was the *Halibut* (SSGN-587) seen here. Originally designed as a diesel-electric-powered submarine, its intended role, as reflected in its prefix designation, was to be a cruise missile-launching platform for the Regulus I or II missiles, a role it performed until 1965. *(US Navy)*

To store its load of Regulus I or II missiles, the *Halibut* (SSGN-587) had a single massive watertight hangar seen here as a quarter-scale wooden mock-up. It encompassed most of the submarine's bow as it had with the two diesel-electric boats of the *Grayback* class, the *Growler* (SSG-557) and *Grayback* (SSG-574) that had two separate hangars. (*US Navy*)

To reduce the noise generated by its nuclear-powered submarines, the US Navy experimented with turbo-electric propulsion instead of the standard steam turbine propulsion on the *Tullibee* (SSN-597), shown here commissioned in November 1960. The experiment did not prove successful and *Tullibee* proved to be a one-of-a-kind design. (*US Navy*)

The *Narwhal* (SSN-671), shown here upon its launching on 12 July 1969, would be a one-of-a-kind design in which the US Navy tested many different internal design concepts. Not all of them lived up to expectations, but those that did appear in subsequent nuclear-powered submarine designs. The US Navy decommissioned the *Narwhal* in July 1999. *(US Navy)*

An important design arrangement that first appeared with the experimental *Tullibee* (SSN-597) was a large spherical sonar array that took up the entire bow of the submarine. With a sizeable sonar array taking up the location of what had traditionally been the location of a submarine's bow torpedo tubes, the US Navy had them relocated amidships on *Tullibee* to fire at a forward angle out of the underside and on follow-on *Permit*-class attack submarines, as shown in this illustration from a Naval manual. *(US Navy)*

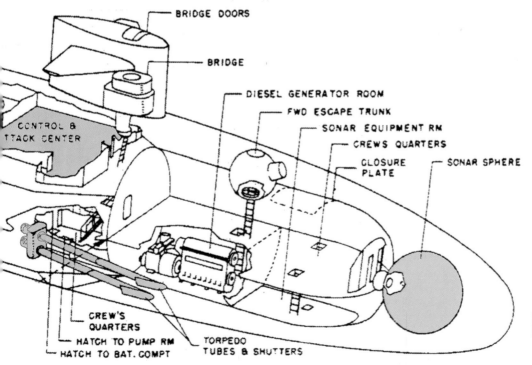

An example of a large spherical sonar with protective covering is seen here going into a *Thresher*-class attack submarine (later renamed the *Permit* class). It has remained a standard design arrangement on all the US Navy's succeeding attack submarine classes. (*US Navy*)

A fibreglass-reinforced plastic sail is going onto the hull of a *Permit*-class attack submarine. In its efforts to increase the speed of the class, thought had been given initially to doing away with the sail altogether to reduce underwater drag. The US Navy rejected that idea. Instead, the size of the sail would be significantly reduced compared to that of previous nuclear-powered attack submarines. (*US Navy*)

The electrically-driven Mk. 37 torpedo pictured here was an active/passive acoustic homing weapon employed from the mid-1950s through to the early 1970s by both US Navy submarines and destroyers. Its primary role was to destroy enemy submarines. The advent of faster and deeper-diving Soviet Navy nuclear submarines rendered it obsolete. *(Paul and Loren Hannah)*

The replacement weapon for the Mk. 14 torpedo and the Mk. 37 torpedo turned out to be the Mk. 48 torpedo. It entered US Navy service in the early 1970s. The current version pictured here is the Mk. 48 ADCAP (Advanced Capabilities) torpedo. When launched, the torpedo can perform programmed search, acquisition and attack procedures and conduct multiple attacks on a selected target if it misses. *(US Navy)*

An artist's impression of a SUBROC (Submarine Rocket) launched from a submerged US Navy nuclear-powered attack submarine. In service aboard US Navy submarines from 1964 to 1989, it had a nuclear warhead and a listed maximum range of 34 miles. The subsonic weapon could be fired from the standard 21in-diameter torpedo tube. (US Navy)

(**Opposite, above**) The Harpoon missile pictured here, launched from a US Navy surface ship, first appeared on the *Permit*-class attack submarines. It remained in service on US Navy submarines until 1997. On board submarines it resided in an encapsulated container and was fired from the existing 21in-diameter torpedo tubes. A fire-and-forget weapon, it has a listed maximum range of 77 miles. (*US Navy*)

(**Opposite, below**) Pictured on the day of its launching is the *Guitarro* (SSN-665), one of thirty-seven *Sturgeon*-class attack submarines commissioned by the US Navy between 1963 and 1975. Instead of having torpedo tubes located on the underside of their hulls as with the preceding *Permit* class, the *Sturgeon* class and all following attack submarine classes have the torpedo tubes angled outward from a compartment behind the bow sonar dome. (*US Navy*)

(**Above**) In this image, we see the control room of a *Sturgeon*-class attack submarine. As they were longer and had a larger sail than the preceding *Permit* class of attack submarines but the same nuclear reactor, they were a few knots slower. On the positive side, ergonomic lessons learned from the *Permit* class were incorporated into the interior spaces of the *Sturgeon* class, making them very comfortable submarines for their crews on long patrols. (*US Navy*)

(**Above**) The last nine examples of the thirty-seven *Sturgeon*-class attack submarines were lengthened by 10ft to accommodate additional electronic equipment. The lengthening also allowed seven of them to transport the removable Dry Deck Shelter (DDS), pictured here, beginning in 1982. The DDS could be employed to carry SEAL Delivery Vehicles (SDVs), Combat Rubber Raiding Craft (CRRC) or a platform to conduct a Mass Swimmer Lock-Out (MSLO). (*US Navy*)

(**Opposite, above**) A new weapon introduced to the *Sturgeon*-class attack submarines in the 1980s is the Tomahawk cruise missile seen here. It is designed to fly at extremely low altitudes at high subsonic speeds, and is directed over an evasive route to its target by various guidance systems. Entering US Navy service in 1983, it continues to serve in many progressively-improved variants. (*US Navy*)

(**Opposite, below**) Carried on board US Navy attack submarines from 1979 through to 2001 was the Mk. 60 Captor Encapsulated Torpedo (configured as a seabed mine) shown here. It could also be deployed by aircraft or surface warships. It consisted of an Mk. 46 Acoustic Homing Torpedo; it would sink to the ocean floor in a vertical position and wait, listen for a target and then swim to engage. (*US Navy*)

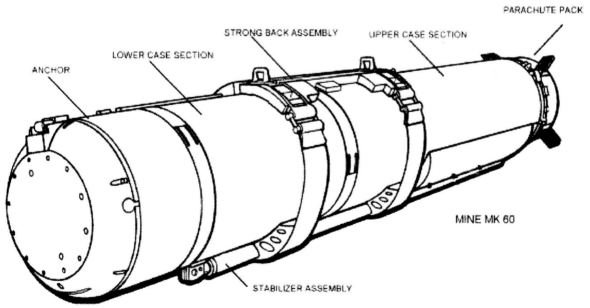

PARACHUTE PACK

STRONG BACK ASSEMBLY   UPPER CASE SECTION

LOWER CASE SECTION

ANCHOR

MINE MK 60

STABILIZER ASSEMBLY

(**Above**) To replace the *Sturgeon*-class attack submarines, the US Navy commissioned sixty-two examples of the *Los Angeles*-class attack submarines such as the one shown here between 1972 and 1996. Of that number, approximately half remain in service as of 2018. Note that the once-standard teardrop submarine shape has been replaced by a tube-like construction. (*US Navy*)

(**Opposite, above**) On this *Los Angeles*-class attack submarine, you can see the large anechoic/decoupling tiles that cover the entire length of the boat. The elastomeric matrix minimizes the structural vibration noise generated by the submarine in the water and defeats the active sonars of other submarines and warships. It does the latter by dissipating incoming sonar waves as they strike the surface. (*US Navy*)

(**Opposite, below**) To locate themselves while transiting the world's oceans, the *Los Angeles*-class attack submarines as seen here depend on their various navigation devices. These include a Navstar Global Positioning System (GPS) receiver. The only caveat with its use is that the submarine must come to periscope depth to fix its position. As a back-up, there is the Ship's Inertial Navigation System (SINS). (*US Navy*)

The crew of a *Los Angeles*-class submarine is shown here preparing to go out on patrol. The sails of the submarines themselves enclose both periscopes and various radar and communication masts. Also there is an array of other sensors within the sails (such as sonars) whose locations can be identified by the various visible panels. (*US Navy*)

The *Los Angeles*-class submarines were divided into three groups by the US Navy. The initial thirty-one boats became known as the first 'flight'. The next eight, or second flight, had a Vertical Launch System (VLS) for twelve Tomahawk missiles fitted in their bows behind their sonar domes as seen here. *(US Navy)*

Pictured here is an example of one of the last twenty-three *Los Angeles*-class submarines built in the third flight. The third flight submarines became known as the *Los Angeles* 'improved' submarines which reflected the more dramatic upgrade between the third flight and the two previous flights. An external spotting feature of the third flight is the lack of diving planes on the sail, having moved to the bow in retractable slots. *(US Navy)*

(**Opposite, above**) In this image we see a *Los Angeles* improved submarine. The long fairing visible on the starboard side of the boat's upper hull is a housing for a towed array sonar. It consists of a steel cable that can be miles long with attached hydrophones. It is deployed, or 'streamed', by the submarine when in the open ocean and retracted when no longer required. (*US Navy*)

(**Opposite, below**) The follow-on to the *Los Angeles*-class attack submarines was originally conceived as the *Seawolf*-class attack submarines of a planned twenty-nine boats. Due to the end of the Cold War in 1991 and rising costs, the US Navy decided that only three examples of the *Seawolf* class would be built. An external spotting feature for the *Seawolf* class is the fairing that streamlines the sail to the hull. (*US Navy*)

(**Above**) Inside the control room of a *Seawolf*-class attack submarine. To reduce noise, starting with the *Skipjack* class, the US Navy had the single propeller of previous nuclear-powered attack submarines replaced by a single propulsor (a water-pump jet). The *Seawolf* class would be the first designed and built by Electric Boat using Computer-Aided Design and Manufacturing (CAD/CAM). (*US Navy*)

The third and final example of the *Seawolf* class of submarines, the *Jimmy Carter* (SSN-23) is shown here rolled out from its assembly bay for the first time on 4 June 2004. The US Navy commissioned the submarine on 19 February 2005. It differed from the two previous *Seawolf*-class submarines as it had an added 100ft hull section referred to as the Multi-Mission Platform (MMP). (*US Navy*)

In the early 1950s, the US Navy began thinking about the requirement for a nuclear-armed ballistic missile. At first, against its will, it would be pushed into working together with the US Army on a liquid propellant missile named the 'Jupiter'. Shown here is a concept drawing of the Jupiter fitted into a modified *Skipjack*-class submarine. (*US Navy*)

In 1956, the US Navy pulled out of the Jupiter missile programme as it had embraced the nuclear-armed solid-fuel propellant missile pictured named the 'Polaris'. To expedite fielding of the new missile, five *Skipjack*-class submarines were modified by extending their hull length by 130ft and installing sixteen missile-launching silos within that space as well as associated command and control equipment.(*Vladimir Yakubov*)

The five *Skipjack*-class attack submarines modified to launch the Polaris missile would be renamed the *George Washington*-class Ballistic-Missile Submarines. The Polaris missile eventually became known as a Submarine-Launched Ballistic Missile (SLBM). Pictured here on its day of commissioning, 13 February 1961, is the *Theodore Roosevelt* (SSBN-600) of the *George Washington* class. (*US Navy*)

In spite of the added space in the 100ft added for the Polaris SLBMs, the designers had a problem fitting in the sixteen Polaris missiles and supporting equipment. The result was a very pronounced fairing over the upper hull from the leading edge of the sail, aft. Pictured here is the *Patrick Henry* (SSN-599). *(US Navy)*

Following the five boats of the *George Washington*-class Ballistic-Missile Submarines there appeared thirty-six more Ballistic-Missile Submarines divided into four different classes. The unofficial but popular name for these forty-one boats was the '41 For Freedom' group. Pictured here is the missile compartment of the *John Adams* (SSBN-620) of the *Lafayette* class. *(US Navy)*

(**Opposite, above**) There were four classes of lengthened submarines in the 41 For Freedom group following the first five *George Washington*-class submarines: the *Ethan Allen*, *Lafayette*, *James Madison* and *Benjamin Franklin* classes. In this picture, we see the *Woodrow Wilson* (SSN-624) of the *Lafayette* class with some of its hydraulically-operated missile silo doors open. (*US Navy*)

(**Opposite, below**) An artist's representation of the last model of the Polaris missile, the 'A3', launched from a 41 For Freedom group submarine. The Polaris missile series was in service with the US Navy from 1961 until 1996. The A3 version of the Polaris had three warheads, all intended to strike the same target, and received the label Multiple Re-Entry Vehicle (MRV). (*US Navy*)

(**Above**) The replacements for the 41 For Freedom boats were eighteen examples of the *Ohio*-class Ballistic-Missile Submarines (SSBN) commissioned between 1981 and 1997. The extreme length of these submarines, at 560ft, is evident in this photograph of the *Tennessee* (SSBN-736) which was commissioned on 17 December 1988. The *Ohio* class has a maximum beam of 42ft. (*US Navy*)

In this image, we see an *Ohio*-class Ballistic-Missile Submarine (SSBN) on the left and the much smaller *Los Angeles*-class attack submarine on the right. In contrast to the *Los Angeles*-class submarines that rise to the surface every so often to visit foreign ports, the *Ohio*-class submarines remain submerged throughout their patrols and seldom even transmit radio messages so as not to reveal their locations. (*US Navy*)

On display here is a mock-up of the US Navy's Submarine-Launched Ballistic Missile (SLBM), named the 'Poseidon'. The authentic missile was armed with a Multiple Independent Targeted Re-Entry Vehicle (MIRV) intended to strike many different targets at approximately the same time. The Poseidon served from 1971 till 1992. Its replacement, the 'Trident' series, began in service in 1979. (*Vladimir Yakubov*)

In flight here is a Trident (SLBM), the replacement for the Poseidon. It is a three-stage, solid-fuel, inertially-guided missile. In an *Ohio*-class Ballistic-Missile Submarine (SSBN) it is launched by the pressure of expanding gas within its launch tube. When the missile reaches the surface, it enters the boost phase and its first, second and third-stage rocket motors ignite, sending it off to its targets. (*US Navy*)

(**Opposite, above**) Within the missile compartment of an *Ohio*-class Ballistic-Missile Submarine (SSBN) a sailor monitors a diagnostic panel. The Trident series missiles within the submarine's launch tubes are 44ft in length with a diameter of 83in and weigh in at approximately 130,000lb. The latest version of the Trident series is known as the Life-Extended Trident II D5 and entered service in 2017. (*US Navy*)

(**Opposite, below**) Pictured here is a young US Navy officer on board an *Ohio*-class Ballistic-Missile Submarine (SSBN) holding the pistol-like trigger for firing a Trident. In wartime, permission to do so comes from shore-based command and control units down through the boat's captain. It then has to be authenticated by the senior officers on board before the trigger can be pulled. (*US Navy*)

(**Above**) An artist's impression of one of the four initial production examples of the *Ohio*-class Strategic Missile Submarines (SSBN) that would be converted into a new platform assigned the label Guided Missile Submarine (SSGN). Each of the SSGNs can support and launch 154 Tomahawk cruise missiles as well as unmanned underwater or aerial vehicles, as well as deploy 66 US Navy SEALs. (*US Navy*)

The Tomahawk cruise missiles on the four *Ohio*-class Guided Missile Submarines (SSGNs) are loaded in seven-shot Multiple-All-Up-Round Canisters (MACs) as seen here. These MACs are in up to twenty-two of the twenty-four missile-launch tubes of the submarine. Instead of the MACs, the missile launch tubes can also accommodate US Navy SEAL equipment. *(US Navy)*

Chapter Five

Post-Cold War Submarines

In need of a replacement for the ageing *Los Angeles*-class attack submarines and as a result of the unaffordable cost of building enough *Seawolf*-class submarines to replace them, in February 1991 the US Navy began designing a new class of more affordable attack submarines. The result would be the *Virginia*-class boats, the first in the US Navy to be designed entirely by computer.

The US Navy decided to divide construction of the *Virginia*-class submarines between Huntington Ingalls Industries Newport News Shipbuilding and General Dynamics Electric Boat. A primary aim of this arrangement was to reduce the financial cost of building the *Virginia*-class boats to a relatively low annual rate in the two shipyards, thus preserving critical submarine-construction skills and the resources at both locations.

Initial plans called for the US Navy to take forty-eight *Virginia*-class submarines into service by 2043. However, the number as of 2019 was thirty examples, with the expectation that this could be increased in the future.

The first *Virginia*-class submarine received its commissioning in October 2004 with the hull classification number SSN-774. As of the end of 2019, the US Navy has sixteen examples in service with their hull classification numbers in numerical sequence. These sixteen consist of three blocks, with each block representing a progressively-improved version of the vessel.

Virginia-*Class Description*

The *Virginia*-class submarines have a surface displacement of 8,700 tons and a length of 377ft. The US Navy lists their submerged top speed as 25 knots or more and test depth of 800ft. Respected sources suggest the submarine's top speed is 35 knots and test depth 1,600ft. Weaponry is configurable based on mission requirements and ranges from torpedoes to Tomahawk cruise missiles as well as mines.

Rather than a single propeller, the *Virginia*-class submarines have a pump jet pro-pulsor system (water jet) that had first appeared on the *Seawolf*-class submarines. One of the key advantages of a pump jet propulsor system for submarines is that the jets are quieter than propellers. The US Navy's newest versions of its torpedoes also use a pump jet propulsor system.

Some of the state-of-the-art design features that came with the *Virginia*-class submarines appear in this passage from an online US Navy fact file:

> The *Virginia* class has several innovations that significantly enhance its warfighting capabilities with an emphasis on littoral operations. *Virginia* class SSNs have a fly-by-wire ship control system that provides improved shallow-water ship handling ... In *Virginia*-class SSNs, traditional periscopes have been supplanted by two photonics masts that host visible and infrared digital cameras atop telescoping arms. With the removal of the barrel periscopes, the ship's control room has been moved down one deck and away from the hull's curvature, affording it more room and an improved layout that provides the commanding officer with enhanced situational awareness.

The *Virginia*-class boats, beginning with the Block V model, will have an additional mid-body section referred to as the Virginia Payload Module (VPM). It contains four large-diameter, vertical launch tubes to store and fire additional Tomahawk cruise missiles or other payloads, such as large-diameter unmanned underwater vehicles (UUVs).

Columbia Class

The *Ohio*-class submarines were designed for an intended forty-two-year lifespan, meaning that the first boat in the class constructed is due to be decommissioned in 2027. The US Navy wants to have the first of twelve planned replacement submarines ready at the same time. A number of options received consideration, as are detailed in this passage from an October 2106 report by the Congressional Research Service:

> Over the last five years, the US Navy – working with U.S. Strategic Command, the Joint Staff and the Office of the Secretary of Defense – has formally examined various options to replace the *Ohio* ballistic missile submarines as they retire beginning in 2027. This analysis included a variety of replacement platform options, including designs based on the highly successful *Virginia*-class attack submarine program and the current *Ohio*-class ballistic missile submarine. In the end, the US Navy elected to pursue a new design that leverages the lessons from *Ohio*, the *Virginia* advances in shipbuilding and improvements in cost-efficiency.

That new submarine class acquired the name *Columbia*. It will be the same length as that of the *Ohio* class. Its estimated surface displacement as of 2014 is 20,815 tons. The yet-to-be-built submarines will have accommodation for a crew of up to 155 personnel. It will also come with a turbo-electric propulsion system.

Unlike the *Ohio*-class submarines that required a mid-life nuclear refuelling, the nuclear reactors on the *Columbia* class will last the lifespan of the boats themselves, intended to be forty years. Instead of the twenty-four SLBM launch tubes found on the *Ohio* class, the *Columbia* class will have only sixteen SLBM launch tubes in addition to torpedo tubes.

As it has with the *Virginia*-class submarines, the US Navy intends that both Huntington Ingalls Industries Newport News Shipbuilding and General Dynamics Electric Boat be involved with the building of the planned *Columbia* class. The construction work was assigned to General Dynamics Electric Boat as of the end of 2018.

An artist's impression of the *Virginia*-class attack submarine before the design and construction phase began. Note that it features the same streamlined sail design as the *Seawolf*-class attack submarines. As of 2019 seventeen examples of the *Virginia* class were in US Navy service with nine under construction and two on order with more planned for the future. (*US Navy*)

Inside a General Dynamics Electric Boat assembly building is seen a *Virginia*-class attack submarine under construction. All are also referred to as the 'SSN-774' class after the hull classification number on the first boat built. The *Virginia* class is supposed to be the affordable replacement for the *Los Angeles*-class attack submarine that the *Seawolf* class did not prove to be, resulting in only three constructed. *(US Navy)*

At a certain point in the process, General Dynamics Electric Boat moves a submarine under construction outside, as is seen here with a *Virginia*-class attack submarine. Reflecting the ever-continuing pace of modern technology, the *Virginia* class has several new features not seen on the previous *Los Angeles* class. These include a fly-by-wire ship control system that provides improved shallow-water handling. (*US Navy*)

From the beginning, the US Navy has sought various methods of keeping costs down on the *Virginia*-class attack submarine. These include use of as many off-the-shelf commercial electronic components as possible, rather than programme-developed specialized and more expensive counterparts. Pictured here is the control room on a *Virginia*-class boat. (*US Navy*)

(**Above**) In this image of the sail of a *Virginia*-class attack submarine, we see the two telescoping photonics masts that contain both visible and infrared digital cameras as well as a laser range-finder that have replaced traditional periscopes. Unlike the latter, the photonics masts do not penetrate the submarine's hull, allowing for the control station to be moved to a roomier location deeper within the pressure hull. (*US Navy*)

(**Opposite, above**) Pictured here are two of the four 21in-diameter torpedo tubes on the *Virginia*-class attack submarines. As was established with the *Sturgeon*-class attack submarines, they are located behind the bow sonar compartment and are angled outward from the hull. Torpedo-loading was more mechanized than in the past, using power-operated devices. The *Virginia* class had storage space for thirty-seven torpedoes. (*US Navy*)

(**Opposite, below**) The first ten examples of the *Virginia*-class attack submarine that fell under the heading of Block I and II models were armed with the Vertical Launch System (VLS) for twelve Tomahawk missiles. Starting with the Block III model of the *Virginia* class, the US Navy had the VLS replaced with two large 87in Virginia Payload Tubes (VPTs), as seen here with two tubes' hydraulically-operated door fully opened. (*US Navy*)

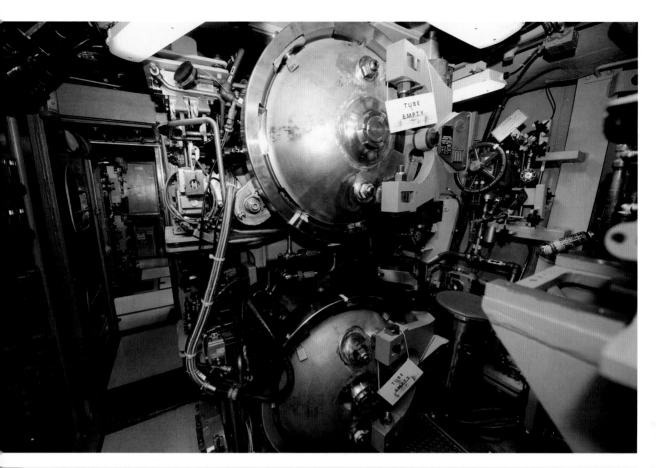

Besides their nuclear reactors, all US Navy nuclear-powered submarines have a back-up diesel engine in case the reactor has to go down for any reason. The engines are a smaller version of the Fairbanks-Morse (FM) diesel engine that drove many of the US Navy fleet boats during the Second World War. Pictured here are crewmen of a *Virginia*-class attack submarine checking the status of their diesel engine. (*US Navy*)

At the very low end of technology in the *Virginia*-class attack submarines are two of the more mundane pieces of equipment seen here: an electrically-powered washing machine and dryer. The submarines have an advanced filtration system and dehumidifiers to maintain not only crew habitability but also optimum conditions for the onboard electronics. (*US Navy*)

Despite the ever-increasing size of US Navy submarines over a century, living quarters for enlisted personnel remain coffin-sized, as seen in this photograph taken inside a *Virginia*-class attack submarine. They are indeed better than the open bunks of Second World War fleet-type boats, with blowers for fresh air, reading lights, bedding and curtains to block most light. (*US Navy*)

Bibliography

Alden, John D., *The Fleet Submarine in the US Navy: Design and Construction History* (Naval Institute Press, 1979).

Christley, Jim, *US Nuclear Submarines: The Fast Attack* (Osprey Publishing, 2007).

Christley, Jim, *US Submarines 1941–1945* (Squadron/Signal Publications, 2006).

Friedman, Norman, *US Submarines Through 1945: An Illustrated Design History* (Naval Institute Press, 1995).

Friedman, Norman, *US Submarines Since 1945: An Illustrated Design History* (Naval Institute Press, 1994).

Friedman, Norman, *US Naval Weapons* (Naval Institute Press, 1985).

Polmar, Norman and Moore, K.J., *Cold War Submarines: The Design and Construction of US and Soviet Submarines* (Potomac Books, 2004).

Stern, Robert C., *US Submarines in Action* (Squadron/Signal Publications, 1979).

Stern, Robert C., *Gato-Class Submarines in Action* (Squadron/Signal Publications, 2009).

Weir, Gary E., *Building American Submarines 1914–1940* (Naval Historical Center, n.d.).